Designed
by
S.H Bando Press

Questions And Customer Service:
email us at bando13press@gmail.com

S.H
BANDO PRESS

This Journal Belongs To

....

The hunger and fullness scale

If you're familiar with (Intuitive Eating), then you know about
the hunger and fullness scale, a toolto help you get in touch with your
hunger and fullness cues.

Here's how to use the HUNGER AND FULLNESS SCALE

When you are getting ready to eat a meal or snack, ask yourself
"Where am I on the hunger and fullness scale?" Ideally, you'll be between a 3
and a 6.(the hunger scale, Choose to scale one meal every day)

Halfway through your meal, pause for 10 seconds, and check in with your
body. Ask again "Where am I on the scale now?"

1 - Painfully hungry (nausea, upset stomach, etc) or sometimes so hungry
 that you don't feel hungry anymore

2 - hangry (moody, cranky, highly irritated) with an empty pit in your
 stomach that doesn't go away and is very distracting

3 - hungry(stomach rumbles, trouble focusing)thought of food more
frequently, feeling like you need energy

4 - I could eat, food thoughts come and go, stomach feels slightly empty

5 - neutral, not hungry or full

6 - stomach feels a little full but not totally satisfied, thoughts of food
less frequent

7 - stomach a little full but a comfortable satisfied, ready to take on your
 next task

8 - full and don't want anything else to eat

9 - change into your yoga pants uncomfortable full or unbutton the top
button kind of full, may feel sleepy

10 - extremely uncomfortably full to the point of nausea feeling sick

How to use:Example

Date: 9/7/2021   Sleep Time: 7 hours   😄 🙂 😐 ☹️ 😣

☕ Breakfast

3 eggs +
spinach

🌮 Lunch

big veggie
salad

🍃 Dinner

chicken lettuce
wraps

🧁 Snack

apple + almond
butter

Water Intake

🥛 🥛 🥛 🥛 🥛 🥛 🥛 🥛 🥛

Hunger Scale

1 2 3 4 ⑤ 6 7 8 9 10

starving   dinner   So Full

I Ate Because

☐ STARVING ☐ CRAVINGS ☒ TROUBLED ☐ MOODY ☐ NEED FUEL

Symptoms/Feelings Post Meal ⟶ How Long After Meal?

☐ STRONG ☒ BLOATING ☐ DIGESTIVE ☐ < 1HOUR ☒ 1 - 2 HOURS

☐ FOCUSED ☐ FOGGY MIND ☐ OTHER

what? where? When? Why?

When I'm hungry, do I think about food repeatedly? When I feel
hungry before lunch, I think about eating frequently,
but before dinner, I don't think about eating much

Date: 2/8/2021   Sleep Time: 7½   😁 🙂 😐 🙁 😣

☕ Breakfast   🌮 Lunch ②   🍲 Dinner ③

None   Egg + Bacon Sandwich
                     Crisps
                     Twirl
                     Orange Juice

🧁 Snack

Water Intake
☑ ☑ ☑ ☑ ☐ ☐ ☐ ☐ ☐

Hunger Scale
1 2 3 4 5 6 7 8 9 10
starving   So Full

I Ate Because
☑ STARVING   ☐ CRAVINGS   ☐ TROUBLED   ☐ MOODY   ☐ NEED FUEL

Symptoms/Feelings Post Meal ——→ How Long After Meal?
☐ STRONG   ☐ BLOATING   ☐ DIGESTIVE   ☐ < 1HOUR   ☐ 1 - 2 HOURS
☐ FOCUSED   ☐ FOGGY MIND   ☐ OTHER

what? where? When? Why?

When I'm hungry, do I think about food repeatedly? Yes

Date: _____ Sleep Time: _____ 😄 🙂 😐 🙁 😣

☕ Breakfast

_____
_____
_____
_____
_____

🌮 Lunch

_____
_____
_____
_____
_____

🍝 Dinner

_____
_____
_____
_____
_____

🧁 Snack

_____
_____
_____
_____

Water Intake

🥛 🥛 🥛 🥛 🥛 🥛 🥛 🥛 🥛

Hunger Scale

1 2 3 4 5 6 7 8 9 10

starving   So Full

I Ate Because

☐ STARVING ☐ CRAVINGS ☐ TROUBLED ☐ MOODY ☐ NEED FUEL

Symptoms/Feelings Post Meal ⟶ How Long After Meal?

☐ STRONG ☐ BLOATING ☐ DIGESTIVE ☐ < 1HOUR ☐ 1 - 2 HOURS

☐ FOCUSED ☐ FOGGY MIND ☐ OTHER _____

what? where? When? Why?

Am I afraid to lose control when I have dinner quickly? _____

_____
_____
_____
_____
_____

Date: _____ Sleep Time: _____ 😄 ☺ 😐 ☹ 😣

Breakfast

_____
_____
_____
_____
_____

Lunch

_____
_____
_____
_____
_____

Dinner

_____
_____
_____
_____
_____

Snack

_____
_____
_____
_____
_____

Water Intake

Hunger Scale

1 2 3 4 5 6 7 8 9 10

starving   So Full

I Ate Because

☐ STARVING ☐ CRAVINGS ☐ TROUBLED ☐ MOODY ☐ NEED FUEL

Symptoms/Feelings Post Meal ⟶ How Long After Meal?

☐ STRONG ☐ BLOATING ☐ DIGESTIVE ☐ < 1HOUR ☐ 1 - 2 HOURS

☐ FOCUSED ☐ FOGGY MIND ☐ OTHER _____

what? where? When? Why?

Which foods seem most appealing? How much of them would
I like to eat? _____

_____
_____
_____
_____

Date: _____ Sleep Time: _____ 😄 🙂 😐 🙁 😣

☕ Breakfast   🌮 Lunch   🥗 Dinner

_____   _____   _____
_____   _____   _____
_____   _____   _____
_____   _____   _____

🧁 Snack

_____
_____
_____
_____

Water Intake

🥛 🥛 🥛 🥛 🥛 🥛 🥛 🥛 🥛

Hunger Scale

1   2   3   4   5   6   7   8   9   10

starving   So Full

I Ate Because

☐ STARVING   ☐ CRAVINGS   ☐ TROUBLED   ☐ MOODY   ☐ NEED FUEL

Symptoms/Feelings Post Meal ⟶ How Long After Meal?

☐ STRONG   ☐ BLOATING   ☐ DIGESTIVE   ☐ < 1HOUR   ☐ 1 - 2 HOURS

☐ FOCUSED   ☐ FOGGY MIND   ☐ OTHER _____

what? where? When? Why?

Bring your focus back to your body and your breathing. How do you feel?

_____
_____
_____
_____
_____

Date: _____   Sleep Time: _____   😄 ☺ 😐 ☹ 😣

☕ Breakfast   🌮 Lunch   🍝 Dinner

_____   _____   _____
_____   _____   _____
_____   _____   _____
_____   _____   _____

🧁 Snack   _____ Water Intake _____

_____   🥛 🥛 🥛 🥛 🥛 🥛 🥛 🥛 🥛
_____
_____   _____ Hunger Scale _____
_____
                          1 2 3 4 5 6 7 8 9 10
                          starving   So Full

_____ I Ate Because _____
☐ STARVING   ☐ CRAVINGS   ☐ TROUBLED   ☐ MOODY   ☐ NEED FUEL

┌─ Symptoms/Feelings Post Meal ──────▶ How Long After Meal? ─┐
│ ☐ STRONG   ☐ BLOATING   ☐ DIGESTIVE   ☐ < 1HOUR   ☐ 1 - 2 HOURS │
│ ☐ FOCUSED   ☐ FOGGY MIND   ☐ OTHER _____ │
└──┘

what? where? When? Why?

Am I still hungry or thirsty? _____

_____
_____
_____
_____

Date: _____   Sleep Time: _____   😄 🙂 😐 ☹️ 😖
_____

☕ Breakfast   🌮 Lunch   🍲 Dinner

_____   _____   _____
_____   _____   _____
_____   _____   _____
_____   _____   _____

🧁 Snack   _____ Water Intake _____

_____   [glass] [glass] [glass] [glass] [glass] [glass] [glass] [glass] [glass]

_____   _____ Hunger Scale _____
_____
_____   1 2 3 4 5 6 7 8 9 10
_____   ├─────────────────────────┤
                                 starving   So Full

_____ I Ate Because _____

☐ STARVING   ☐ CRAVINGS   ☐ TROUBLED   ☐ MOODY   ☐ NEED FUEL

┌ Symptoms/Feelings Post Meal ──────⟶ How Long After Meal? ─┐

☐ STRONG   ☐ BLOATING   ☐ DIGESTIVE   ☐ < 1HOUR   ☐ 1 - 2 HOURS

☐ FOCUSED   ☐ FOGGY MIND ☐ OTHER

what? where? When? Why?

(Today) Do I really need to eat any more? _____

_____
_____
_____
_____

Date: _____ Sleep Time: _____ 😄 ☺ 😐 ☹ 😣

☕ Breakfast

_____
_____
_____
_____
_____

🌮 Lunch

_____
_____
_____
_____
_____

🍽 Dinner

_____
_____
_____
_____
_____

🧁 Snack

_____
_____
_____
_____
_____

Water Intake

🥛 🥛 🥛 🥛 🥛 🥛 🥛 🥛 🥛

Hunger Scale

1 2 3 4 5 6 7 8 9 10

starving   So Full

I Ate Because

☐ STARVING ☐ CRAVINGS ☐ TROUBLED ☐ MOODY ☐ NEED FUEL

Symptoms/Feelings Post Meal ⟶ How Long After Meal?

☐ STRONG ☐ BLOATING ☐ DIGESTIVE ☐ < 1HOUR ☐ 1 - 2 HOURS

☐ FOCUSED ☐ FOGGY MIND ☐ OTHER _____

what? where? When? Why?

Where do I think My food comes from? _____
_____
_____
_____
_____

Date: _____ Sleep Time: _____ 😄 🙂 😐 ☹️ 😣

☕ Breakfast   🌮 Lunch   🥗 Dinner

_____   _____   _____
_____   _____   _____
_____   _____   _____
_____   _____   _____
_____   _____   _____

🧁 Snack

_____
_____
_____
_____

Water Intake

Hunger Scale

1 2 3 4 5 6 7 8 9 10

starving   So Full

I Ate Because

☐ STARVING   ☐ CRAVINGS   ☐ TROUBLED   ☐ MOODY   ☐ NEED FUEL

Symptoms/Feelings Post Meal ⟶ How Long After Meal?

☐ STRONG   ☐ BLOATING   ☐ DIGESTIVE   ☐ < 1HOUR   ☐ 1 - 2 HOURS

☐ FOCUSED   ☐ FOGGY MIND   ☐ OTHER _____

what? where? When? Why?

How does my food grow, and what do I think it needs to help it grow?

_____
_____
_____
_____
_____

Date:_____ Sleep Time:_____ 😄 🙂 😐 🙁 😣

Breakfast

_____
_____
_____
_____
_____

Lunch

_____
_____
_____
_____
_____

Dinner

_____
_____
_____
_____
_____

Snack

_____
_____
_____
_____
_____

Water Intake

🥛 🥛 🥛 🥛 🥛 🥛 🥛 🥛 🥛

Hunger Scale

1 2 3 4 5 6 7 8 9 10

starving   So Full

I Ate Because

☐ STARVING ☐ CRAVINGS ☐ TROUBLED ☐ MOODY ☐ NEED FUEL

Symptoms/Feelings Post Meal ⟶ How Long After Meal?

☐ STRONG ☐ BLOATING ☐ DIGESTIVE ☐ < 1HOUR ☐ 1 - 2 HOURS

☐ FOCUSED ☐ FOGGY MIND ☐ OTHER _____

what? where? When? Why?

What exercises did I use and how well did they work? _____
_____
_____
_____
_____

Date: _____ Sleep Time: _____ 😄 🙂 😐 🙁 😣

☕ Breakfast

_____
_____
_____
_____
_____

🌮 Lunch

_____
_____
_____
_____
_____

🍝 Dinner

_____
_____
_____
_____
_____

🧁 Snack

_____
_____
_____
_____

Water Intake

🥛 🥛 🥛 🥛 🥛 🥛 🥛 🥛 🥛

Hunger Scale

1 2 3 4 5 6 7 8 9 10
starving   So Full

I Ate Because

☐ STARVING   ☐ CRAVINGS   ☐ TROUBLED   ☐ MOODY   ☐ NEED FUEL

Symptoms/Feelings Post Meal ———➤ How Long After Meal?

☐ STRONG   ☐ BLOATING   ☐ DIGESTIVE   ☐ < 1HOUR   ☐ 1-2 HOURS

☐ FOCUSED   ☐ FOGGY MIND   ☐ OTHER

what? where? When? Why?

If I were going to eat or drink something right now, what is my hungry for? What is it thirsty for? _____

_____
_____
_____
_____

Date: _____ Sleep Time: _____ 😄 ☺ 😐 🙁 😣

☕ Breakfast   🌮 Lunch   🍝 Dinner

_____   _____   _____
_____   _____   _____
_____   _____   _____
_____   _____   _____
_____   _____   _____

🧁 Snack

_____
_____
_____
_____
_____

Water Intake

Hunger Scale

1   2   3   4   5   6   7   8   9   10

starving   So Full

I Ate Because

☐ STARVING   ☐ CRAVINGS   ☐ TROUBLED   ☐ MOODY   ☐ NEED FUEL

Symptoms/Feelings Post Meal ➔ How Long After Meal?

☐ STRONG   ☐ BLOATING   ☐ DIGESTIVE   ☐ < 1HOUR   ☐ 1 - 2 HOURS

☐ FOCUSED   ☐ FOGGY MIND   ☐ OTHER _____

what? where? When? Why?

When do I feel like eating? _____

_____
_____
_____
_____

Date: _____ Sleep Time: _____ 😄 🙂 😐 🙁 😣
_____

☕ Breakfast   🌮 Lunch   🍳 Dinner

_____   _____   _____
_____   _____   _____
_____   _____   _____
_____   _____   _____
_____   _____   _____

🧁 Snack

_____   _____ Water Intake _____
_____
_____   [glass][glass][glass][glass][glass][glass][glass][glass][glass]
_____
_____   _____ Hunger Scale _____

                    1 2 3 4 5 6 7 8 9 10
                    |—————————————————————————|
                    starving   So Full

_____ I Ate Because _____

☐ STARVING   ☐ CRAVINGS   ☐ TROUBLED   ☐ MOODY   ☐ NEED FUEL

── Symptoms/Feelings Post Meal ──➤ How Long After Meal? ──

☐ STRONG   ☐ BLOATING   ☐ DIGESTIVE   ☐ < 1HOUR   ☐ 1-2 HOURS

☐ FOCUSED   ☐ FOGGY MIND   ☐ OTHER

what? where? When? Why?

What is driving my eating at any given time? _____

_____
_____
_____
_____

Date: _____   Sleep Time: _____   😄 🙂 😐 🙁 😣

☕ Breakfast

_____
_____
_____
_____
_____

🌮 Lunch

_____
_____
_____
_____
_____

🍝 Dinner

_____
_____
_____
_____
_____

🧁 Snack

_____
_____
_____
_____

Water Intake

🥛 🥛 🥛 🥛 🥛 🥛 🥛 🥛 🥛

Hunger Scale

1 2 3 4 5 6 7 8 9 10

starving   So Full

I Ate Because

☐ STARVING   ☐ CRAVINGS   ☐ TROUBLED   ☐ MOODY   ☐ NEED FUEL

Symptoms/Feelings Post Meal ➜ How Long After Meal?

☐ STRONG   ☐ BLOATING   ☐ DIGESTIVE   ☐ < 1HOUR   ☐ 1 - 2 HOURS

☐ FOCUSED   ☐ FOGGY MIND   ☐ OTHER _____

what? where? When? Why?

How do I get the food I have chosen into my body? _____
_____
_____
_____
_____
_____

Date: _____ Sleep Time: _____ 😄 🙂 😐 ☹️ 😣

Breakfast

_____
_____
_____
_____
_____

Lunch

_____
_____
_____
_____
_____

Dinner

_____
_____
_____
_____
_____

Snack

_____
_____
_____
_____

Water Intake

Hunger Scale

1	2	3	4	5	6	7	8	9	10

starving   So Full

I Ate Because

☐ STARVING ☐ CRAVINGS ☐ TROUBLED ☐ MOODY ☐ NEED FUEL

Symptoms/Feelings Post Meal ⟶ How Long After Meal?

☐ STRONG ☐ BLOATING ☐ DIGESTIVE ☐ < 1HOUR ☐ 1-2 HOURS

☐ FOCUSED ☐ FOGGY MIND ☐ OTHER

what? where? When? Why?

How did I feel today before the meals? _____

_____
_____
_____
_____

Date: _____ Sleep Time: _____ 😄 🙂 😐 🙁 😣

☕ Breakfast   🌮 Lunch   🍝 Dinner

_____   _____   _____
_____   _____   _____
_____   _____   _____
_____   _____   _____
_____   _____   _____

🧁 Snack

_____

_____

_____

_____

Water Intake

🥛 🥛 🥛 🥛 🥛 🥛 🥛 🥛 🥛

Hunger Scale

1   2   3   4   5   6   7   8   9   10
starving   So Full

I Ate Because

☐ STARVING   ☐ CRAVINGS   ☐ TROUBLED   ☐ MOODY   ☐ NEED FUEL

Symptoms/Feelings Post Meal ——→ How Long After Meal?

☐ STRONG   ☐ BLOATING   ☐ DIGESTIVE   ☐ < 1HOUR   ☐ 1 - 2 HOURS

☐ FOCUSED   ☐ FOGGY MIND ☐ OTHER _____

what? where? When? Why?

can I describe the eating environment at work? _____

_____
_____
_____
_____
_____

Date: _____ Sleep Time: _____ 😄 🙂 😐 ☹️ 😣

☕ Breakfast   🌮 Lunch   🍽 Dinner
_____   _____   _____
_____   _____   _____
_____   _____   _____
_____   _____   _____
_____   _____   _____

🧁 Snack

_____   Water Intake _____
_____
_____   🥛 🥛 🥛 🥛 🥛 🥛 🥛 🥛 🥛
_____
_____   Hunger Scale _____

                     1 2 3 4 5 6 7 8 9 10
                     |—————————————————————————————|
                     starving   So Full

I Ate Because
☐ STARVING   ☐ CRAVINGS   ☐ TROUBLED   ☐ MOODY   ☐ NEED FUEL

Symptoms/Feelings Post Meal ————➤ How Long After Meal?
☐ STRONG   ☐ BLOATING   ☐ DIGESTIVE   ☐ < 1HOUR   ☐ 1-2 HOURS
☐ FOCUSED   ☐ FOGGY MIND   ☐ OTHER _____

what? where? When? Why?

What are at four things I don't eat mindfully at lunch or when having
dinner? _____

- _____
- _____
- _____
- _____

Date:_____ Sleep Time:_____ 😄 ☺ 😐 ☹ 😖

☕ Breakfast   🌮 Lunch   🍽 Dinner

_____   _____   _____
_____   _____   _____
_____   _____   _____
_____   _____   _____
_____   _____   _____

🧁 Snack

_____

_____   Water Intake

_____   [glass][glass][glass][glass][glass][glass][glass][glass][glass]

_____   Hunger Scale

_____   1 2 3 4 5 6 7 8 9 10
                      starving   So Full

─── I Ate Because ───
☐ STARVING ☐ CRAVINGS ☐ TROUBLED ☐ MOODY ☐ NEED FUEL

─ Symptoms/Feelings Post Meal ──→ How Long After Meal? ─
☐ STRONG   ☐ BLOATING   ☐ DIGESTIVE ☐ < 1HOUR   ☐ 1 - 2 HOURS
☐ FOCUSED   ☐ FOGGY MIND ☐ OTHER _____

what? where? When? Why?

Where do I eat (at home)? _____
_____
_____
_____
_____

Date: _____ Sleep Time: _____ 😄 🙂 😐 🙁 😣

☕ Breakfast

_____
_____
_____
_____
_____

🌮 Lunch

_____
_____
_____
_____
_____

🍽 Dinner

_____
_____
_____
_____
_____

🧁 Snack

_____
_____
_____
_____

Water Intake

🥛 🥛 🥛 🥛 🥛 🥛 🥛 🥛 🥛

Hunger Scale

1 2 3 4 5 6 7 8 9 10
starving   So Full

I Ate Because

☐ STARVING   ☐ CRAVINGS   ☐ TROUBLED   ☐ MOODY   ☐ NEED FUEL

Symptoms/Feelings Post Meal ⟶ How Long After Meal?

☐ STRONG   ☐ BLOATING   ☐ DIGESTIVE   ☐ < 1HOUR   ☐ 1-2 HOURS
☐ FOCUSED   ☐ FOGGY MIND   ☐ OTHER _____

what? where? When? Why?

Today while eating (lunch), Am I busy or calm? _____

_____
_____
_____
_____
_____

Date: _____ Sleep Time: _____ 😄 🙂 😐 🙁 😣

☕ Breakfast   🌮 Lunch   🍽 Dinner

_____   _____   _____
_____   _____   _____
_____   _____   _____
_____   _____   _____
_____   _____   _____

🧁 Snack

_____
_____
_____
_____
_____

Water Intake

🥛 🥛 🥛 🥛 🥛 🥛 🥛 🥛 🥛

Hunger Scale

1   2   3   4   5   6   7   8   9   10

starving   So Full

I Ate Because

☐ STARVING   ☐ CRAVINGS   ☐ TROUBLED   ☐ MOODY   ☐ NEED FUEL

Symptoms/Feelings Post Meal → How Long After Meal?

☐ STRONG   ☐ BLOATING   ☐ DIGESTIVE   ☐ < 1HOUR   ☐ 1 - 2 HOURS

☐ FOCUSED   ☐ FOGGY MIND   ☐ OTHER _____

what? where? When? Why?

What types of foods that I prevent myself from eating? _____

_____
_____
_____
_____

Date: _____ Sleep Time: _____ 😄 🙂 😐 🙁 😣
_____

☕ Breakfast   🌮 Lunch   🍤 Dinner

_____   _____   _____
_____   _____   _____
_____   _____   _____
_____   _____   _____
_____   _____   _____

🧁 Snack   ———————— Water Intake ————————
                         ┌───┐
_____   │ 🥛 🥛 🥛 🥛 🥛 🥛 🥛 🥛 🥛 │
                         └───┘
_____
                         ———————— Hunger Scale ————————
_____   ┌───┐
                         │ 1 2 3 4 5 6 7 8 9 10   │
_____   │ |————————————————————————   │
                         │ starving   So Full   │
                         └───┘

———————————————— I Ate Because ————————————————
┌───┐
│ ☐ STARVING ☐ CRAVINGS ☐ TROUBLED ☐ MOODY ☐ NEED FUEL │
└───┘

┌── Symptoms/Feelings Post Meal ———➤ How Long After Meal? ──┐
│ ☐ STRONG   ☐ BLOATING   ☐ DIGESTIVE   ☐ < 1HOUR ☐ 1- 2 HOURS │
│   │
│ ☐ FOCUSED ☐ FOGGY MIND ☐ OTHER _____ │
└───┘

what? where? When? Why?

Do I feel guilty when I eat foods that I previously refrained from? _____

_____
_____
_____
_____

Date: _____ Sleep Time: _____ 😄 🙂 😐 🙁 😣

☕ Breakfast

_____
_____
_____
_____

🌮 Lunch

_____
_____
_____
_____

🍤 Dinner

_____
_____
_____
_____

🧁 Snack

_____
_____
_____
_____

Water Intake

🥛 🥛 🥛 🥛 🥛 🥛 🥛 🥛 🥛

Hunger Scale

1   2   3   4   5   6   7   8   9   10

starving   So Full

I Ate Because

☐ STARVING ☐ CRAVINGS ☐ TROUBLED ☐ MOODY ☐ NEED FUEL

Symptoms/Feelings Post Meal ➔ How Long After Meal?

☐ STRONG ☐ BLOATING ☐ DIGESTIVE ☐ < 1HOUR ☐ 1 - 2 HOURS

☐ FOCUSED ☐ FOGGY MIND ☐ OTHER _____

what? where? When? Why?

Am I afraid to lose control when I have lunch quickly? _____

_____
_____
_____
_____

Date: _____ Sleep Time: _____ 😄 🙂 😐 ☹️ 😖

☕ **Breakfast**

_____
_____
_____
_____

🌮 **Lunch**

_____
_____
_____
_____

🥗 **Dinner**

_____
_____
_____
_____

🧁 **Snack**

_____
_____
_____
_____

Water Intake

[🥛] [🥛] [🥛] [🥛] [🥛] [🥛] [🥛] [🥛] [🥛]

Hunger Scale

1 2 3 4 5 6 7 8 9 10

starving   So Full

I Ate Because

☐ STARVING ☐ CRAVINGS ☐ TROUBLED ☐ MOODY ☐ NEED FUEL

Symptoms/Feelings Post Meal ➞ How Long After Meal?

☐ STRONG ☐ BLOATING ☐ DIGESTIVE ☐ < 1HOUR ☐ 1 - 2 HOURS

☐ FOCUSED ☐ FOGGY MIND ☐ OTHER _____

what? where? When? Why?

(At work)Do I eat fast, barely eating my food? why? _____

_____
_____
_____
_____
_____

Date:_____   Sleep Time:_____   😄 ☺ 😐 ☹ 😫

☕ **Breakfast**   🌮 **Lunch**   🥗 **Dinner**

_____   _____   _____
_____   _____   _____
_____   _____   _____
_____   _____   _____
_____   _____   _____

🧁 **Snack**   ──── Water Intake ────

_____   🥛 🥛 🥛 🥛 🥛 🥛 🥛 🥛 🥛
_____
_____   ──── Hunger Scale ────
_____
_____   1 2 3 4 5 6 7 8 9 10
                         starving   So Full

──── I Ate Because ────

☐ STARVING   ☐ CRAVINGS   ☐ TROUBLED   ☐ MOODY   ☐ NEED FUEL

Symptoms/Feelings Post Meal ──────▶ How Long After Meal?

☐ STRONG   ☐ BLOATING   ☐ DIGESTIVE   ☐ < 1HOUR   ☐ 1 - 2 HOURS

☐ FOCUSED   ☐ FOGGY MIND ☐ OTHER _____

what? where? When? Why?

What emotions trigger me to overeat? _____

_____
_____
_____
_____
_____

Date: _____ Sleep Time: _____ 😄 🙂 😐 ☹️ 😣
_____

☕ Breakfast   🌮 Lunch   🍃 Dinner

_____   _____   _____
....
_____   _____   _____
....
_____   _____   _____
....

🧁 Snack   _____ Water Intake _____

_____   [glass][glass][glass][glass][glass][glass][glass][glass][glass]
....
_____   _____ Hunger Scale _____
....
_____   1 2 3 4 5 6 7 8 9 10
....
_____   starving   So Full
....

_____ I Ate Because _____

☐ STARVING   ☐ CRAVINGS   ☐ TROUBLED   ☐ MOODY   ☐ NEED FUEL

Symptoms/Feelings Post Meal ⟶ How Long After Meal?

☐ STRONG   ☐ BLOATING   ☐ DIGESTIVE   ☐ < 1HOUR   ☐ 1-2 HOURS

☐ FOCUSED   ☐ FOGGY MIND   ☐ OTHER _____

what? where? When? Why?

Do I have a plan to refrain from eating beside the computer or watching
TV? What's the plan? _____

_____
....
_____
....
_____

Date:_____ Sleep Time: _____ 😁 ☺ 😐 ☹ 😣

☕ Breakfast   🌮 Lunch   🍲 Dinner

_____   _____   _____
_____   _____   _____
_____   _____   _____
_____   _____   _____
_____   _____   _____

🧁 Snack   Water Intake

_____   [glass] [glass] [glass] [glass] [glass] [glass] [glass] [glass] [glass]

_____   Hunger Scale

_____   1   2   3   4   5   6   7   8   9   10

_____   starving   So Full

_____

                    I Ate Because
☐ STARVING   ☐ CRAVINGS   ☐ TROUBLED   ☐ MOODY   ☐ NEED FUEL

Symptoms/Feelings Post Meal ⟶ How Long After Meal?
☐ STRONG   ☐ BLOATING   ☐ DIGESTIVE   ☐ < 1HOUR   ☐ 1 - 2 HOURS
☐ FOCUSED   ☐ FOGGY MIND ☐ OTHER _____

what? where? When? Why?

Do I exercise? What exercises do I would prefer? _____
_____
_____
_____
_____
_____

Date: _____ Sleep Time: _____ 😄 🙂 😐 ☹️ 😣

☕ Breakfast   🌮 Lunch   🍽️ Dinner

_____   _____   _____
_____   _____   _____
_____   _____   _____
_____   _____   _____

🧁 Snack

_____

_____

_____

Water Intake

[ ] [ ] [ ] [ ] [ ] [ ] [ ] [ ] [ ]

Hunger Scale

1 2 3 4 5 6 7 8 9 10

starving   So Full

I Ate Because

☐ STARVING   ☐ CRAVINGS   ☐ TROUBLED   ☐ MOODY   ☐ NEED FUEL

Symptoms/Feelings Post Meal ➔ How Long After Meal?

☐ STRONG   ☐ BLOATING   ☐ DIGESTIVE   ☐ < 1HOUR   ☐ 1 - 2 HOURS

☐ FOCUSED   ☐ FOGGY MIND   ☐ OTHER _____

what? where? When? Why?

How many times a day do I feel so hungry? _____

_____

_____

_____

_____

Date:_____ Sleep Time:_____ 😄 🙂 😐 🙁 😣

☕ Breakfast   🌮 Lunch   🍝 Dinner

_____   _____   _____
_____   _____   _____
_____   _____   _____
_____   _____   _____
_____   _____   _____

🧁 Snack

_____

_____ Water Intake _____

🥛 🥛 🥛 🥛 🥛 🥛 🥛 🥛 🥛

_____ Hunger Scale _____

1   2   3   4   5   6   7   8   9   10

starving   So Full

_____ I Ate Because _____

☐ STARVING   ☐ CRAVINGS   ☐ TROUBLED   ☐ MOODY   ☐ NEED FUEL

Symptoms/Feelings Post Meal ➡ How Long After Meal?

☐ STRONG   ☐ BLOATING   ☐ DIGESTIVE   ☐ < 1HOUR   ☐ 1 - 2 HOURS

☐ FOCUSED   ☐ FOGGY MIND ☐ OTHER _____

what? where? When? Why?

Did I try to cut out some meals during the day? _____

_____

_____

_____

_____

Date: _____ Sleep Time: _____ 😄 🙂 😐 🙁 😣

_____

☕ Breakfast   🌮 Lunch   🍝 Dinner

_____   _____   _____
_____   _____   _____
_____   _____   _____
_____   _____   _____
_____   _____   _____

🧁 Snack   ——— Water Intake ———
_____   [⌷ ⌷ ⌷ ⌷ ⌷ ⌷ ⌷ ⌷ ⌷]
_____
_____   ——— Hunger Scale ———
_____   1 2 3 4 5 6 7 8 9 10
_____   starving   So Full
_____

——— I Ate Because ———

☐ STARVING   ☐ CRAVINGS   ☐ TROUBLED   ☐ MOODY   ☐ NEED FUEL

┌ Symptoms/Feelings Post Meal ———→ How Long After Meal? ┐

☐ STRONG   ☐ BLOATING   ☐ DIGESTIVE   ☐ < 1HOUR   ☐ 1-2 HOURS

☐ FOCUSED   ☐ FOGGY MIND ☐ OTHER _____

what? where? When? Why?

Write down health problems you can have while eating certain foods

• _____
• _____
• _____
• _____
• _____

Date: _____   Sleep Time: _____   😄 🙂 😐 🙁 😣

☕ Breakfast

_____
_____
_____
_____
_____

🌮 Lunch

_____
_____
_____
_____
_____

🍽 Dinner

_____
_____
_____
_____
_____

🧁 Snack

_____
_____
_____
_____
_____

Water Intake

🥛 🥛 🥛 🥛 🥛 🥛 🥛 🥛 🥛

Hunger Scale

1 2 3 4 5 6 7 8 9 10
starving   So Full

I Ate Because

☐ STARVING ☐ CRAVINGS ☐ TROUBLED ☐ MOODY ☐ NEED FUEL

Symptoms/Feelings Post Meal ⟶ How Long After Meal?

☐ STRONG ☐ BLOATING ☐ DIGESTIVE ☐ < 1HOUR ☐ 1 - 2 HOURS

☐ FOCUSED ☐ FOGGY MIND ☐ OTHER _____

what? where? When? Why?

What are four healthy foods that help me feel better? _____

_____
_____
_____
_____
_____

Date: _____ Sleep Time: _____ 😄 🙂 😐 ☹️ 😣

☕ Breakfast   🌮 Lunch   🍽️ Dinner

---------------   ---------------   ---------------
---------------   ---------------   ---------------
---------------   ---------------   ---------------
---------------   ---------------   ---------------
---------------   ---------------   ---------------

🧁 Snack

Water Intake

Hunger Scale

1 2 3 4 5 6 7 8 9 10

starving   So Full

I Ate Because

☐ STARVING   ☐ CRAVINGS   ☐ TROUBLED   ☐ MOODY   ☐ NEED FUEL

Symptoms/Feelings Post Meal ⟶ How Long After Meal?

☐ STRONG   ☐ BLOATING   ☐ DIGESTIVE   ☐ < 1HOUR   ☐ 1 - 2 HOURS

☐ FOCUSED   ☐ FOGGY MIND   ☐ OTHER

what? where? When? Why?

What specific change would I make to improve my diet? _____

_____

_____

_____

_____

Date: _____   Sleep Time: _____   😄 ☺ 😐 ☹ 😣

☕ Breakfast

_____
_____
_____
_____
_____

🌮 Lunch

_____
_____
_____
_____
_____

🍝 Dinner

_____
_____
_____
_____
_____

🧁 Snack

_____
_____
_____
_____

Water Intake

🥛 🥛 🥛 🥛 🥛 🥛 🥛 🥛 🥛

Hunger Scale

1   2   3   4   5   6   7   8   9   10

starving   So Full

I Ate Because

☐ STARVING   ☐ CRAVINGS   ☐ TROUBLED   ☐ MOODY   ☐ NEED FUEL

Symptoms/Feelings Post Meal ➡ How Long After Meal?

☐ STRONG   ☐ BLOATING   ☐ DIGESTIVE   ☐ < 1HOUR   ☐ 1 - 2 HOURS

☐ FOCUSED   ☐ FOGGY MIND   ☐ OTHER _____

what? where? When? Why?

What emotions trigger me to not overeat? _____
_____
_____
_____
_____
_____

Date: _____ Sleep Time: _____ 😄 🙂 😐 🙁 😣

☕ Breakfast   🌮 Lunch   🍃 Dinner

_____   _____   _____
_____   _____   _____
_____   _____   _____
_____   _____   _____

🧁 Snack

_____   ——— Water Intake ———
_____   [🥛][🥛][🥛][🥛][🥛][🥛][🥛][🥛][🥛]
_____
_____   ——— Hunger Scale ———
_____
                  1 2 3 4 5 6 7 8 9 10
                  ⊢————————————————————————⊣
                  starving   So Full

——— I Ate Because ———

☐ STARVING   ☐ CRAVINGS   ☐ TROUBLED   ☐ MOODY   ☐ NEED FUEL

— Symptoms/Feelings Post Meal ——→ How Long After Meal? —

☐ STRONG   ☐ BLOATING   ☐ DIGESTIVE   ☐ < 1HOUR   ☐ 1-2 HOURS

☐ FOCUSED   ☐ FOGGY MIND ☐ OTHER _____

what? where? When? Why?

When was the last time I feel painfully hungry (nausea, stomach upset, etc.)?

_____

_____

_____

_____

_____

Date:_____ Sleep Time:_____ 😄 ☺ 😐 ☹ 😣

☕ Breakfast   🌮 Lunch   🍽 Dinner

_____   _____   _____
_____   _____   _____
_____   _____   _____
_____   _____   _____
_____   _____   _____

🧁 Snack   ———— Water Intake ————

_____   [🥛 🥛 🥛 🥛 🥛 🥛 🥛 🥛 🥛]
_____
_____   ———— Hunger Scale ————
_____
_____   1 2 3 4 5 6 7 8 9 10
                      |————————————————————————|
                      starving   So Full

———————————— I Ate Because ————————————
☐ STARVING ☐ CRAVINGS ☐ TROUBLED ☐ MOODY ☐ NEED FUEL

— Symptoms/Feelings Post Meal ——→ How Long After Meal? —
☐ STRONG   ☐ BLOATING   ☐ DIGESTIVE   ☐ < 1HOUR   ☐ 1 - 2 HOURS
☐ FOCUSED   ☐ FOGGY MIND ☐ OTHER _____

what? where? When? Why?

How much fuel do I consume? _____
_____
_____
_____
_____
_____

Date: _____ Sleep Time: _____ 😄 🙂 😐 🙁 😣

☕ Breakfast

_____
_____
_____
_____
_____

🌮 Lunch

_____
_____
_____
_____
_____

🍃 Dinner

_____
_____
_____
_____
_____

🧁 Snack

_____
_____
_____
_____

Water Intake

🥛 🥛 🥛 🥛 🥛 🥛 🥛 🥛 🥛

Hunger Scale

1 2 3 4 5 6 7 8 9 10

starving   So Full

I Ate Because

☐ STARVING ☐ CRAVINGS ☐ TROUBLED ☐ MOODY ☐ NEED FUEL

Symptoms/Feelings Post Meal ⟶ How Long After Meal?

☐ STRONG ☐ BLOATING ☐ DIGESTIVE ☐ < 1HOUR ☐ 1 - 2 HOURS

☐ FOCUSED ☐ FOGGY MIND ☐ OTHER _____

what? where? When? Why?

Where do I invest the energy I consume? _____
_____
_____
_____
_____
_____

Date: _____ Sleep Time: _____ 😄 ☺ 😐 ☹ 😖

☕ Breakfast   🌮 Lunch   🥗 Dinner

_____   _____   _____
_____   _____   _____
_____   _____   _____
_____   _____   _____
_____

🧁 Snack

_____
_____
_____
_____
_____

Water Intake

[glass] [glass] [glass] [glass] [glass] [glass] [glass] [glass] [glass]

Hunger Scale

1 2 3 4 5 6 7 8 9 10

starving   So Full

I Ate Because

☐ STARVING   ☐ CRAVINGS   ☐ TROUBLED   ☐ MOODY   ☐ NEED FUEL

Symptoms/Feelings Post Meal ⟶ How Long After Meal?

☐ STRONG   ☐ BLOATING   ☐ DIGESTIVE   ☐ < 1HOUR   ☐ 1 - 2 HOURS

☐ FOCUSED   ☐ FOGGY MIND ☐ OTHER _____

what? where? When? Why?

How did I feel today after the meals? _____

_____
_____
_____
_____
_____

Date: _____ Sleep Time: _____ 😄 ☺ 😐 ☹ 😖

☕ Breakfast   🌮 Lunch   🍝 Dinner

_____   _____   _____
_____   _____   _____
_____   _____   _____
_____   _____   _____

🧁 Snack

_____

Water Intake

🥛 🥛 🥛 🥛 🥛 🥛 🥛 🥛 🥛

Hunger Scale

1   2   3   4   5   6   7   8   9   10

starving   So Full

I Ate Because

☐ STARVING   ☐ CRAVINGS   ☐ TROUBLED   ☐ MOODY   ☐ NEED FUEL

Symptoms/Feelings Post Meal ➡️ **How Long After Meal?**

☐ STRONG   ☐ BLOATING   ☐ DIGESTIVE   ☐ < 1HOUR   ☐ 1-2 HOURS

☐ FOCUSED   ☐ FOGGY MIND   ☐ OTHER _____

what? where? When? Why?

Today while eating (breakfast), Am I busy or calm? _____

_____
_____
_____
_____
_____

Date: _____ Sleep Time: _____ ☺ ☺ ☺ ☹ ☹

☕ Breakfast   🌮 Lunch   🍽 Dinner

_____   _____   _____
_____   _____   _____
_____   _____   _____
_____   _____   _____
_____   _____   _____

🧁 Snack   _____ Water Intake _____

_____   ▢ ▢ ▢ ▢ ▢ ▢ ▢ ▢ ▢
_____
_____   _____ Hunger Scale _____
_____
_____   1 2 3 4 5 6 7 8 9 10
_____   ├────────────────────────┤
                           starving   So Full

_____ I Ate Because _____
☐ STARVING ☐ CRAVINGS ☐ TROUBLED ☐ MOODY ☐ NEED FUEL

┌ Symptoms/Feelings Post Meal ───────▶ How Long After Meal? ┐
☐ STRONG   ☐ BLOATING   ☐ DIGESTIVE   ☐ < 1HOUR ☐ 1 - 2 HOURS
☐ FOCUSED   ☐ FOGGY MIND ☐ OTHER _____

what? where? When? Why?

When was the last time I was extremely uncomfortably full to the point
of nausea feeling sick? _____

_____
_____
_____
_____

Date: _____ Sleep Time: _____ 😄 🙂 😐 🙁 😣

☕ Breakfast   🌮 Lunch   🍽 Dinner

_____   _____   _____
_____   _____   _____
_____   _____   _____
_____   _____   _____
_____   _____   _____

🧁 Snack

_____

_____

_____

_____

Water Intake

[glass] [glass] [glass] [glass] [glass] [glass] [glass] [glass] [glass]

Hunger Scale

1 2 3 4 5 6 7 8 9 10

starving   So Full

I Ate Because

☐ STARVING   ☐ CRAVINGS   ☐ TROUBLED   ☐ MOODY   ☐ NEED FUEL

Symptoms/Feelings Post Meal ——→ How Long After Meal?

☐ STRONG   ☐ BLOATING   ☐ DIGESTIVE   ☐ < 1HOUR   ☐ 1 - 2 HOURS

☐ FOCUSED   ☐ FOGGY MIND   ☐ OTHER _____

what? where? When? Why?

(While Eating) Anytime the stomach feels a little full but not completely
satisfied? _____

_____

_____

_____

Date: _____   Sleep Time: _____   😄 ☺ 😐 ☹ 😣

☕ Breakfast

_____
_____
_____
_____
_____

🌮 Lunch

_____
_____
_____
_____
_____

🍝 Dinner

_____
_____
_____
_____
_____

🧁 Snack

_____
_____
_____
_____
_____

Water Intake

🥛 🥛 🥛 🥛 🥛 🥛 🥛 🥛 🥛

Hunger Scale

1 2 3 4 5 6 7 8 9 10
starving   So Full

I Ate Because

☐ STARVING   ☐ CRAVINGS   ☐ TROUBLED   ☐ MOODY   ☐ NEED FUEL

Symptoms/Feelings Post Meal ➔ How Long After Meal?

☐ STRONG   ☐ BLOATING   ☐ DIGESTIVE   ☐ < 1HOUR   ☐ 1 - 2 HOURS

☐ FOCUSED   ☐ FOGGY MIND   ☐ OTHER _____

what? where? When? Why?

When I'm hungry, Do I have trouble concentrating? _____

_____
_____
_____
_____

Date: _____ Sleep Time: _____ 😄 🙂 😐 🙁 😣

☕ Breakfast
_____
_____
_____
_____

🌮 Lunch
_____
_____
_____
_____

🍝 Dinner
_____
_____
_____
_____

🧁 Snack
_____
_____
_____
_____

Water Intake

🥛 🥛 🥛 🥛 🥛 🥛 🥛 🥛 🥛

Hunger Scale

1 2 3 4 5 6 7 8 9 10

starving   So Full

I Ate Because

☐ STARVING ☐ CRAVINGS ☐ TROUBLED ☐ MOODY ☐ NEED FUEL

Symptoms/Feelings Post Meal ⟶ How Long After Meal?

☐ STRONG ☐ BLOATING ☐ DIGESTIVE ☐ < 1HOUR ☐ 1 - 2 HOURS

☐ FOCUSED ☐ FOGGY MIND ☐ OTHER _____

what? where? When? Why?

How do I protect myself from the influence of food that can deplete
my energy (high sugar food, Greasy food, Etc)? _____

_____
_____
_____
_____

Date:_____ Sleep Time:_____ 😄 ☺ 😐 ☹ 😫

☕ Breakfast   🌮 Lunch   🍽 Dinner

_____   _____   _____
_____   _____   _____
_____   _____   _____
_____   _____   _____
_____   _____   _____

🧁 Snack   Water Intake

_____

[9 glasses]

_____

_____   Hunger Scale

_____   1 2 3 4 5 6 7 8 9 10
_____ |————————————————————————|
_____   starving   So Full

I Ate Because

☐ STARVING ☐ CRAVINGS ☐ TROUBLED ☐ MOODY ☐ NEED FUEL

Symptoms/Feelings Post Meal ——→ How Long After Meal?

☐ STRONG   ☐ BLOATING   ☐ DIGESTIVE   ☐ < 1HOUR ☐ 1 - 2 HOURS

☐ FOCUSED   ☐ FOGGY MIND ☐ OTHER _____

what? where? When? Why?

What are at four things I don't eat mindfully at breakfast or when having a snack? _____

- _____
- _____
- _____
- _____

Date: _____ Sleep Time: _____ 😄 🙂 😐 🙁 😣

☕ Breakfast

_____
_____
_____
_____
_____

🌮 Lunch

_____
_____
_____
_____
_____

🍽 Dinner

_____
_____
_____
_____
_____

🧁 Snack

_____
_____
_____
_____

Water Intake

[ ] [ ] [ ] [ ] [ ] [ ] [ ] [ ] [ ]

Hunger Scale

1   2   3   4   5   6   7   8   9   10

starving   So Full

I Ate Because

[ ] STARVING [ ] CRAVINGS [ ] TROUBLED [ ] MOODY [ ] NEED FUEL

Symptoms/Feelings Post Meal ⟶ How Long After Meal?

[ ] STRONG   [ ] BLOATING   [ ] DIGESTIVE   [ ] < 1HOUR   [ ] 1 - 2 HOURS

[ ] FOCUSED [ ] FOGGY MIND [ ] OTHER

what? where? When? Why?

What scares me (about my health)? _____

_____
_____
_____
_____

Date: _____   Sleep Time: _____   😄 🙂 😐 🙁 😖

☕ Breakfast

_____
_____
_____
_____
_____

🌮 Lunch

_____
_____
_____
_____
_____

🍲 Dinner

_____
_____
_____
_____
_____

🧁 Snack

_____
_____
_____
_____
_____

Water Intake

🥛 🥛 🥛 🥛 🥛 🥛 🥛 🥛 🥛

Hunger Scale

1 2 3 4 5 6 7 8 9 10

starving   So Full

I Ate Because

☐ STARVING ☐ CRAVINGS ☐ TROUBLED ☐ MOODY ☐ NEED FUEL

Symptoms/Feelings Post Meal ——→ **How Long After Meal?**

☐ STRONG ☐ BLOATING ☐ DIGESTIVE ☐ < 1HOUR ☐ 1 - 2 HOURS

☐ FOCUSED ☐ FOGGY MIND ☐ OTHER _____

what? where? When? Why?

If there are any negative consequences, or fears, related to achieving
a healthy diet, what would it be? _____

_____
_____
_____
_____

Date: _____ Sleep Time: _____ 😄 🙂 😐 🙁 😣

☕ Breakfast

_____
_____
_____
_____
_____

🌮 Lunch

_____
_____
_____
_____
_____

🍽 Dinner

_____
_____
_____
_____
_____

🧁 Snack

_____
_____
_____
_____

Water Intake

🥛 🥛 🥛 🥛 🥛 🥛 🥛 🥛 🥛

Hunger Scale

1 2 3 4 5 6 7 8 9 10

starving   So Full

I Ate Because

☐ STARVING ☐ CRAVINGS ☐ TROUBLED ☐ MOODY ☐ NEED FUEL

Symptoms/Feelings Post Meal ⟶ How Long After Meal?

☐ STRONG ☐ BLOATING ☐ DIGESTIVE   ☐ < 1HOUR ☐ 1 - 2 HOURS

☐ FOCUSED ☐ FOGGY MIND ☐ OTHER _____

what? where? When? Why?

What single and achievable commitment can I make to improve
my self-care? _____
_____
_____
_____
_____

Date: _____   Sleep Time: _____   😄 ☺ 😐 ☹ 😣

☕ Breakfast   🌮 Lunch   🍝 Dinner
_____   _____   _____
_____   _____   _____
_____   _____   _____
_____   _____   _____
_____   _____   _____

🧁 Snack   Water Intake
_____   🥛 🥛 🥛 🥛 🥛 🥛 🥛 🥛 🥛
_____
                               Hunger Scale
_____   1 2 3 4 5 6 7 8 9 10
_____   starving   So Full

_____ I Ate Because _____
☐ STARVING   ☐ CRAVINGS   ☐ TROUBLED   ☐ MOODY   ☐ NEED FUEL

┌─ Symptoms/Feelings Post Meal ──────→ How Long After Meal? ─┐
☐ STRONG   ☐ BLOATING   ☐ DIGESTIVE   ☐ < 1HOUR   ☐ 1 - 2 HOURS
☐ FOCUSED   ☐ FOGGY MIND ☐ OTHER _____

what? where? When? Why?

When I feel pain emotional - the best thing I can do for myself : _____
_____
_____
_____
_____

Date: _____ Sleep Time: _____ 😄 🙂 😐 ☹️ 😖

☕ Breakfast _____ 🌮 Lunch _____ 🍝 Dinner

_____   _____   _____
_____   _____   _____
_____   _____   _____
_____   _____   _____

🧁 Snack

_____

_____ Water Intake _____

[ ] [ ] [ ] [ ] [ ] [ ] [ ] [ ] [ ]

_____ Hunger Scale _____

1 2 3 4 5 6 7 8 9 10

starving   So Full

_____ I Ate Because _____

☐ STARVING   ☐ CRAVINGS   ☐ TROUBLED   ☐ MOODY   ☐ NEED FUEL

Symptoms/Feelings Post Meal ⟶ How Long After Meal?

☐ STRONG   ☐ BLOATING   ☐ DIGESTIVE   ☐ < 1HOUR   ☐ 1 - 2 HOURS

☐ FOCUSED   ☐ FOGGY MIND   ☐ OTHER _____

what? where? When? Why?

List the questions you need to answer urgently : _____

- _____
- _____
- _____
- _____
- _____

Date: _____ Sleep Time: _____ 😄 ☺ 😐 ☹ 😣

☕ Breakfast

_____
_____
_____
_____
_____

🌮 Lunch

_____
_____
_____
_____
_____

🍝 Dinner

_____
_____
_____
_____
_____

🧁 Snack

_____
_____
_____
_____

Water Intake

🥛 🥛 🥛 🥛 🥛 🥛 🥛 🥛 🥛

Hunger Scale

1 2 3 4 5 6 7 8 9 10

starving   So Full

I Ate Because

☐ STARVING   ☐ CRAVINGS   ☐ TROUBLED   ☐ MOODY   ☐ NEED FUEL

Symptoms/Feelings Post Meal ⟶ How Long After Meal?

☐ STRONG   ☐ BLOATING   ☐ DIGESTIVE   ☐ < 1HOUR   ☐ 1 - 2 HOURS

☐ FOCUSED   ☐ FOGGY MIND   ☐ OTHER _____

what? where? When? Why?

How do I hesitate to take action on what I can eat? _____

_____
_____
_____
_____
_____

Date: _____ Sleep Time: _____ 😄 🙂 😐 🙁 😣

☕ Breakfast

_____
_____
_____
_____
_____

🌮 Lunch

_____
_____
_____
_____
_____

🍝 Dinner

_____
_____
_____
_____
_____

🧁 Snack

_____
_____
_____
_____

Water Intake

🥛 🥛 🥛 🥛 🥛 🥛 🥛 🥛 🥛

Hunger Scale

1 2 3 4 5 6 7 8 9 10

starving   So Full

I Ate Because

☐ STARVING   ☐ CRAVINGS   ☐ TROUBLED   ☐ MOODY   ☐ NEED FUEL

Symptoms/Feelings Post Meal ——→ How Long After Meal?

☐ STRONG   ☐ BLOATING   ☐ DIGESTIVE   ☐ < 1HOUR   ☐ 1 - 2 HOURS

☐ FOCUSED   ☐ FOGGY MIND   ☐ OTHER _____

what? where? When? Why?

What are the foods I don't eat mindfully at lunch (at work)? _____

_____
_____
_____
_____

Date:_____ Sleep Time:_____ 😄 ☺ 😐 ☹ 😩

☕ Breakfast   🌮 Lunch   🍽 Dinner

_____   _____   _____
_____   _____   _____
_____   _____   _____
_____   _____   _____

🧁 Snack

_____

_____

_____

_____

Water Intake

[glass] [glass] [glass] [glass] [glass] [glass] [glass] [glass] [glass]

Hunger Scale

1 2 3 4 5 6 7 8 9 10

starving   So Full

I Ate Because

☐ STARVING   ☐ CRAVINGS   ☐ TROUBLED   ☐ MOODY   ☐ NEED FUEL

Symptoms/Feelings Post Meal ⟶ How Long After Meal?

☐ STRONG   ☐ BLOATING   ☐ DIGESTIVE   ☐ < 1HOUR   ☐ 1 - 2 HOURS

☐ FOCUSED   ☐ FOGGY MIND ☐ OTHER _____

what? where? When? Why?

What five things would I like to change most about myself ? _____

- _____
- _____
- _____
- _____
- _____

Date: _____   Sleep Time: _____   😄 ☺ 😐 ☹ 😖

☕ Breakfast   🌮 Lunch   🍽 Dinner

_____   _____   _____
_____   _____   _____
_____   _____   _____
_____   _____   _____
_____   _____   _____

🧁 Snack

_____   _____ Water Intake _____
_____
_____   🥛 🥛 🥛 🥛 🥛 🥛 🥛 🥛 🥛
_____
_____   _____ Hunger Scale _____

                         1   2   3   4   5   6   7   8   9   10
                         ├──────────────────────────────────┤
                         starving   So Full

_____ I Ate Because _____

☐ STARVING   ☐ CRAVINGS   ☐ TROUBLED   ☐ MOODY   ☐ NEED FUEL

┌ Symptoms/Feelings Post Meal ──────⟶ How Long After Meal? ┐

☐ STRONG   ☐ BLOATING   ☐ DIGESTIVE   ☐ < 1HOUR   ☐ 1- 2 HOURS

☐ FOCUSED   ☐ FOGGY MIND   ☐ OTHER _____

what? where? When? Why?

If my body could speak, he would say : _____
_____
_____
_____
_____

Date: _____   Sleep Time: _____   😄 ☺ 😐 ☹ 😣

☕ Breakfast   🌮 Lunch   🍝 Dinner

_____   _____   _____
_____   _____   _____
_____   _____   _____
_____   _____   _____

🧁 Snack

Water Intake

🥛 🥛 🥛 🥛 🥛 🥛 🥛 🥛 🥛

Hunger Scale

1 2 3 4 5 6 7 8 9 10

starving   So Full

I Ate Because

☐ STARVING ☐ CRAVINGS ☐ TROUBLED ☐ MOODY ☐ NEED FUEL

Symptoms/Feelings Post Meal ⟶ How Long After Meal?

☐ STRONG ☐ BLOATING ☐ DIGESTIVE ☐ < 1HOUR ☐ 1 - 2 HOURS

☐ FOCUSED ☐ FOGGY MIND ☐ OTHER _____

what? where? When? Why?

If I can change one thing in my diet, what should I change and why ?

_____
_____
_____
_____

Date: _____ Sleep Time: _____ 😄 🙂 😐 ☹️ 😣

☕ Breakfast   🌮 Lunch   🍳 Dinner

_____   _____   _____
_____   _____   _____
_____   _____   _____
_____   _____   _____

🧁 Snack

_____   ———— Water Intake ————————————————————
_____   [glass][glass][glass][glass][glass][glass][glass][glass][glass]
_____
_____   ———— Hunger Scale ————————

                            1 2 3 4 5 6 7 8 9 10
                            |————————————————————————|
                            starving   So Full

———————— I Ate Because ————————
☐ STARVING   ☐ CRAVINGS   ☐ TROUBLED   ☐ MOODY   ☐ NEED FUEL

— Symptoms/Feelings Post Meal ——➤ How Long After Meal? —
☐ STRONG   ☐ BLOATING   ☐ DIGESTIVE   ☐ < 1HOUR   ☐ 1-2 HOURS
☐ FOCUSED   ☐ FOGGY MIND ☐ OTHER _____

what? where? When? Why?

What are my favorite ways to take care of myself physically
and emotionally? _____

_____
_____
_____
_____

Date: _____ Sleep Time: _____ 😄 ☺ 😐 ☹ 😣

☕ Breakfast

_____
_____
_____
_____

🌮 Lunch

_____
_____
_____
_____

🥗 Dinner

_____
_____
_____
_____

🧁 Snack

_____
_____
_____
_____

———— Water Intake ————

🥛 🥛 🥛 🥛 🥛 🥛 🥛 🥛 🥛

———— Hunger Scale ————

1 2 3 4 5 6 7 8 9 10

starving   So Full

———— I Ate Because ————

☐ STARVING ☐ CRAVINGS ☐ TROUBLED ☐ MOODY ☐ NEED FUEL

┌ Symptoms/Feelings Post Meal ——→ How Long After Meal? ┐

☐ STRONG   ☐ BLOATING   ☐ DIGESTIVE   ☐ < 1HOUR   ☐ 1 - 2 HOURS

☐ FOCUSED ☐ FOGGY MIND ☐ OTHER _____

what? where? When? Why?

Am I ready to leave eating (high-sugar food, fatty food, etc.)? _____

_____
_____
_____
_____

Date: _____ Sleep Time: _____ 😄 🙂 😐 ☹️ 😣

☕ **Breakfast**

_____
_____
_____
_____
_____

🥗 **Lunch**

_____
_____
_____
_____
_____

🍲 **Dinner**

_____
_____
_____
_____
_____

🧁 **Snack**

_____
_____
_____
_____

—— **Water Intake** ——

🥛 🥛 🥛 🥛 🥛 🥛 🥛 🥛 🥛

—— **Hunger Scale** ——

1 2 3 4 5 6 7 8 9 10

starving   So Full

—— **I Ate Because** ——

☐ STARVING ☐ CRAVINGS ☐ TROUBLED ☐ MOODY ☐ NEED FUEL

— **Symptoms/Feelings Post Meal** ——→ **How Long After Meal?** —

☐ STRONG ☐ BLOATING ☐ DIGESTIVE   ☐ < 1HOUR ☐ 1--2 HOURS

☐ FOCUSED ☐ FOGGY MIND ☐ OTHER _____

what? where? When? Why?

How do I feel responsible for my health? _____

_____
_____
_____
_____
_____

Date: _____ Sleep Time: _____ 😄 🙂 😐 ☹️ 😣

☕ **Breakfast**   🌮 **Lunch**   🥗 **Dinner**

_____   _____   _____
_____   _____   _____
_____   _____   _____
_____   _____   _____
_____   _____   _____

🧁 **Snack**

_____
_____
_____
_____
_____
_____

Water Intake

🥛 🥛 🥛 🥛 🥛 🥛 🥛 🥛 🥛

Hunger Scale

1   2   3   4   5   6   7   8   9   10
starving   So Full

I Ate Because

☐ STARVING   ☐ CRAVINGS   ☐ TROUBLED   ☐ MOODY   ☐ NEED FUEL

Symptoms/Feelings Post Meal ➔ **How Long After Meal?**

☐ STRONG   ☐ BLOATING   ☐ DIGESTIVE   ☐ < 1HOUR   ☐ 1 - 2 HOURS
☐ FOCUSED   ☐ FOGGY MIND   ☐ OTHER _____

what? where? When? Why?

If I have extra weight, what are the five things that cause that ? _____

- _____
- _____
- _____
- _____
- _____

Date: _____ Sleep Time: _____ 😄 🙂 😐 🙁 😣

☕ Breakfast   🌮 Lunch   🍲 Dinner

_____   _____   _____
_____   _____   _____
_____   _____   _____
_____   _____   _____
_____   _____   _____

🧁 Snack

_____

—————————————— Water Intake ——————————————

🥛 🥛 🥛 🥛 🥛 🥛 🥛 🥛 🥛

_____

—————————————— Hunger Scale ——————————————

1 2 3 4 5 6 7 8 9 10

starving   So Full

——————————— I Ate Because ———————————

☐ STARVING   ☐ CRAVINGS   ☐ TROUBLED   ☐ MOODY   ☐ NEED FUEL

— Symptoms/Feelings Post Meal ——→ How Long After Meal? —

☐ STRONG   ☐ BLOATING   ☐ DIGESTIVE   ☐ < 1HOUR   ☐ 1 - 2 HOURS

☐ FOCUSED   ☐ FOGGY MIND   ☐ OTHER _____

what? where? When? Why?

On a scale of 1 to 10, where am I when it comes to being calm and focused in difficult situations ? ——————————————————

_____

_____

_____

_____

Date: _____ Sleep Time: _____ 😁 ☺ 😐 ☹ 😣

☕ Breakfast

_____
_____
_____
_____
_____

🍲 Lunch

_____
_____
_____
_____
_____

🍳 Dinner

_____
_____
_____
_____
_____

🧁 Snack

_____
_____
_____
_____
_____

Water Intake

[ ] [ ] [ ] [ ] [ ] [ ] [ ] [ ] [ ]

Hunger Scale

1　2　3　4　5　6　7　8　9　10

starving   So Full

I Ate Because

☐ STARVING　☐ CRAVINGS　☐ TROUBLED　☐ MOODY　☐ NEED FUEL

Symptoms/Feelings Post Meal ➔ How Long After Meal?

☐ STRONG　☐ BLOATING　☐ DIGESTIVE　☐ < 1HOUR　☐ 1 - 2 HOURS

☐ FOCUSED　☐ FOGGY MIND　☐ OTHER _____

what? where? When? Why?

What prevents me from giving up unhealthy food ? _____

_____
_____
_____
_____

Date: _____ Sleep Time: _____ 😄 🙂 😐 🙁 😣

☕ Breakfast   🌮 Lunch   🍜 Dinner

_____   _____   _____
_____   _____   _____
_____   _____   _____
_____   _____   _____
_____   _____   _____

🧁 Snack

_____   ___ Water Intake ___
_____   🥛 🥛 🥛 🥛 🥛 🥛 🥛 🥛 🥛
_____   ___ Hunger Scale ___
_____   1 2 3 4 5 6 7 8 9 10
                       starving   So Full

___ I Ate Because ___
☐ STARVING ☐ CRAVINGS ☐ TROUBLED ☐ MOODY ☐ NEED FUEL

— Symptoms/Feelings Post Meal ——→ How Long After Meal? —
☐ STRONG ☐ BLOATING ☐ DIGESTIVE   ☐ < 1HOUR ☐ 1 - 2 HOURS
☐ FOCUSED ☐ FOGGY MIND ☐ OTHER _____

what? where? When? Why?

What is the foods that makes me wake up at night?_____
_____
_____
_____
_____
_____

Date: _____ Sleep Time: _____ 😄 🙂 😐 🙁 😖

☕ Breakfast   🌮 Lunch   🥗 Dinner

_____   _____   _____
_____   _____   _____
_____   _____   _____
_____   _____   _____
_____   _____   _____

🧁 Snack   ——— Water Intake ———

_____   [ ] [ ] [ ] [ ] [ ] [ ] [ ] [ ] [ ]
_____
_____   ——— Hunger Scale ———
_____
_____   1 2 3 4 5 6 7 8 9 10
                           starving   So Full

——— I Ate Because ———

☐ STARVING ☐ CRAVINGS ☐ TROUBLED ☐ MOODY ☐ NEED FUEL

⌐ Symptoms/Feelings Post Meal ——→ How Long After Meal? ⌐

☐ STRONG   ☐ BLOATING   ☐ DIGESTIVE   ☐ < 1HOUR   ☐ 1 - 2 HOURS

☐ FOCUSED ☐ FOGGY MIND ☐ OTHER _____

what? where? When? Why?

How do I feel when I enforce a healthy diet? _____

_____
_____
_____
_____

Date: _____ Sleep Time: _____ 😁 ☺ 😐 ☹ 😣

☕ Breakfast

_____
_____
_____
_____
_____

🍔 Lunch

_____
_____
_____
_____
_____

🍜 Dinner

_____
_____
_____
_____
_____

🧁 Snack

_____
_____
_____
_____

Water Intake

🥛 🥛 🥛 🥛 🥛 🥛 🥛 🥛 🥛

Hunger Scale

1 2 3 4 5 6 7 8 9 10

starving   So Full

I Ate Because

☐ STARVING   ☐ CRAVINGS   ☐ TROUBLED   ☐ MOODY   ☐ NEED FUEL

Symptoms/Feelings Post Meal ⟶ How Long After Meal?

☐ STRONG   ☐ BLOATING   ☐ DIGESTIVE   ☐ < 1HOUR   ☐ 1 - 2 HOURS

☐ FOCUSED   ☐ FOGGY MIND   ☐ OTHER _____

what? where? When? Why?

What are three things I can do regularly to reduce stress? _____

_____
_____
_____
_____
_____

Date: _____ Sleep Time: _____ 😄 ☺ 😐 ☹ 😣

☕ **Breakfast**

_____

_____

_____

_____

_____

🌮 **Lunch**

_____

_____

_____

_____

_____

🍃 **Dinner**

_____

_____

_____

_____

_____

🧁 **Snack**

_____

_____

_____

_____

_____

_____

——— Water Intake ———

🥛 🥛 🥛 🥛 🥛 🥛 🥛 🥛 🥛

——— Hunger Scale ———

1 2 3 4 5 6 7 8 9 10

starving   So Full

——————— I Ate Because ———————

☐ STARVING   ☐ CRAVINGS   ☐ TROUBLED   ☐ MOODY   ☐ NEED FUEL

— Symptoms/Feelings Post Meal ———→ How Long After Meal? —

☐ STRONG   ☐ BLOATING   ☐ DIGESTIVE   ☐ < 1HOUR   ☐ 1 - 2 HOURS

☐ FOCUSED   ☐ FOGGY MIND   ☐ OTHER _____

what? where? When? Why?

What actions can I take to get closer to, or acquire the things
I need to grow? _____

_____

_____

_____

_____

Date: _____ Sleep Time: _____ 😄 🙂 😐 🙁 😣

☕ Breakfast   🌮 Lunch   🍃 Dinner

_____   _____   _____
_____   _____   _____
_____   _____   _____
_____   _____   _____
_____   _____   _____

🧁 Snack

_____   ———— Water Intake ————
_____   [🥛 🥛 🥛 🥛 🥛 🥛 🥛 🥛 🥛]
_____
_____   ———— Hunger Scale ————
_____   1 2 3 4 5 6 7 8 9 10
                     starving   So Full

———— I Ate Because ————
☐ STARVING   ☐ CRAVINGS   ☐ TROUBLED   ☐ MOODY   ☐ NEED FUEL

— Symptoms/Feelings Post Meal ——➤ How Long After Meal? —
☐ STRONG   ☐ BLOATING   ☐ DIGESTIVE   ☐ < 1HOUR   ☐ 1-2 HOURS
☐ FOCUSED   ☐ FOGGY MIND   ☐ OTHER _____

what? where? When? Why?

What are the things I want to pay closer attention to this year? _____

_____
_____
_____
_____
_____

Date: _____ Sleep Time: _____ 😁 🙂 😐 🙁 😣

☕ Breakfast   🌮 Lunch   🍳 Dinner

_____   _____   _____
_____   _____   _____
_____   _____   _____
_____   _____   _____
_____   _____   _____

🧁 Snack

_____

_____ Water Intake _____

⬜ ⬜ ⬜ ⬜ ⬜ ⬜ ⬜ ⬜ ⬜

_____

_____ Hunger Scale _____

1   2   3   4   5   6   7   8   9   10

starving   So Full

_____ I Ate Because _____

☐ STARVING   ☐ CRAVINGS   ☐ TROUBLED   ☐ MOODY   ☐ NEED FUEL

Symptoms/Feelings Post Meal ⟶ How Long After Meal?

☐ STRONG   ☐ BLOATING   ☐ DIGESTIVE   ☐ < 1HOUR   ☐ 1 - 2 HOURS

☐ FOCUSED   ☐ FOGGY MIND ☐ OTHER _____

what? where? When? Why?

Do I feel and express enough gratitude and appreciation for what I have?

_____
_____
_____
_____

Date: _____ Sleep Time: _____ 😄 🙂 😐 🙁 😣

☕ Breakfast   🌮 Lunch   🍜 Dinner

_____   _____   _____
_____   _____   _____
_____   _____   _____
_____   _____   _____
_____   _____   _____

🧁 Snack   ──── Water Intake ────

_____   🥛 🥛 🥛 🥛 🥛 🥛 🥛 🥛 🥛
_____
_____   ──── Hunger Scale ────
_____
_____   1 2 3 4 5 6 7 8 9 10
_____   starving   So Full

──────── I Ate Because ────────

☐ STARVING ☐ CRAVINGS ☐ TROUBLED ☐ MOODY ☐ NEED FUEL

─ Symptoms/Feelings Post Meal ──→ How Long After Meal? ─

☐ STRONG   ☐ BLOATING   ☐ DIGESTIVE   ☐ < 1HOUR ☐ 1-2 HOURS

☐ FOCUSED   ☐ FOGGY MIND ☐ OTHER _____

what? where? When? Why?

What enjoyable activity do I not engage in often enough? _____

_____
_____
_____
_____
_____

Date:_____   Sleep Time:_____   😁 ☺ 😐 ☹ 😣

☕ Breakfast   🌮 Lunch   🍝 Dinner

_____   _____   _____
_____   _____   _____
_____   _____   _____
_____   _____   _____
_____   _____   _____

🧁 Snack   ──── Water Intake ────

_____   [ ] [ ] [ ] [ ] [ ] [ ] [ ] [ ] [ ]
_____
_____   ──── Hunger Scale ────
_____
_____   1 2 3 4 5 6 7 8 9 10
                           starving   So Full

──── I Ate Because ────

☐ STARVING   ☐ CRAVINGS   ☐ TROUBLED   ☐ MOODY   ☐ NEED FUEL

┌ Symptoms/Feelings Post Meal ────→ How Long After Meal? ┐

☐ STRONG   ☐ BLOATING   ☐ DIGESTIVE   ☐ < 1HOUR   ☐ 1 - 2 HOURS

☐ FOCUSED   ☐ FOGGY MIND   ☐ OTHER _____

what? where? When? Why?

How do I feel when I have extremely uncomfortably full? ──────

_____
_____
_____
_____
_____

Date: _____ Sleep Time: _____ 😄 ☺ 😐 🙁 😣

☕ Breakfast

_____
_____
_____
_____
_____

🌮 Lunch

_____
_____
_____
_____
_____

🍲 Dinner

_____
_____
_____
_____
_____

🧁 Snack

_____
_____
_____
_____

Water Intake

🥛 🥛 🥛 🥛 🥛 🥛 🥛 🥛 🥛

Hunger Scale

1   2   3   4   5   6   7   8   9   10

starving   So Full

I Ate Because

☐ STARVING   ☐ CRAVINGS   ☐ TROUBLED   ☐ MOODY   ☐ NEED FUEL

Symptoms/Feelings Post Meal ➔ **How Long After Meal?**

☐ STRONG   ☐ BLOATING   ☐ DIGESTIVE   ☐ < 1HOUR   ☐ 1 - 2 HOURS

☐ FOCUSED   ☐ FOGGY MIND   ☐ OTHER _____

what? where? When? Why?

Am I holding onto (food) that would be better to let go of ? _____

_____
_____
_____
_____
_____

Date: _____ Sleep Time: _____ 😄 ☺ 😐 🙁 😣

☕ Breakfast

_____
_____
_____
_____
_____

🌮 Lunch

_____
_____
_____
_____
_____

🍤 Dinner

_____
_____
_____
_____
_____

🧁 Snack

_____
_____
_____
_____
_____

—— Water Intake ——

⊔ ⊔ ⊔ ⊔ ⊔ ⊔ ⊔ ⊔ ⊔

—— Hunger Scale ——

1 2 3 4 5 6 7 8 9 10

starving   So Full

—————— I Ate Because ——————

☐ STARVING ☐ CRAVINGS ☐ TROUBLED ☐ MOODY ☐ NEED FUEL

— Symptoms/Feelings Post Meal ——➤ How Long After Meal? —

☐ STRONG ☐ BLOATING ☐ DIGESTIVE ☐ < 1HOUR ☐ 1 - 2 HOURS

☐ FOCUSED ☐ FOGGY MIND ☐ OTHER _____

what? where? When? Why?

I feel lively when _____
_____
_____
_____
_____
_____

Date: _____   Sleep Time: _____   😄 🙂 😐 ☹️ 😣

☕ Breakfast   🌮 Lunch   🍃 Dinner

_____   _____   _____
_____   _____   _____
_____   _____   _____
_____   _____   _____
_____   _____   _____

🧁 Snack   _____ Water Intake _____

_____   [glass] [glass] [glass] [glass] [glass] [glass] [glass] [glass] [glass]
_____
_____   _____ Hunger Scale _____
_____
                           1   2   3   4   5   6   7   8   9   10
                           starving   So Full

_____ I Ate Because _____

☐ STARVING   ☐ CRAVINGS   ☐ TROUBLED   ☐ MOODY   ☐ NEED FUEL

Symptoms/Feelings Post Meal ———→ How Long After Meal?

☐ STRONG   ☐ BLOATING   ☐ DIGESTIVE   ☐ < 1HOUR   ☐ 1 - 2 HOURS

☐ FOCUSED   ☐ FOGGY MIND ☐ OTHER _____

what? where? When? Why?

Do I have enough support from friends and family to help me achieve
the personal growth I desire? _____

_____
_____
_____
_____

Date: _____ Sleep Time: _____ 😁 🙂 😐 🙁 😣

☕ Breakfast   🥙 Lunch   🍳 Dinner

_____   _____   _____
_____   _____   _____
_____   _____   _____
_____   _____   _____
_____   _____   _____

🧁 Snack

_____   ___ Water Intake ___

_____   🥛 🥛 🥛 🥛 🥛 🥛 🥛 🥛 🥛

_____   ___ Hunger Scale ___

_____   1   2   3   4   5   6   7   8   9   10
_____   starving   So Full

___ I Ate Because ___

☐ STARVING   ☐ CRAVINGS   ☐ TROUBLED   ☐ MOODY   ☐ NEED FUEL

Symptoms/Feelings Post Meal ⟶ How Long After Meal?

☐ STRONG   ☐ BLOATING   ☐ DIGESTIVE   ☐ < 1HOUR   ☐ 1 - 2 HOURS

☐ FOCUSED   ☐ FOGGY MIND   ☐ OTHER _____

what? where? When? Why?

What am I most proud of ? _____
_____
_____
_____
_____
_____

Date: _____   Sleep Time: _____   😄 🙂 😐 🙁 😣

☕ Breakfast

_____
_____
_____
_____
_____

🌮 Lunch

_____
_____
_____
_____
_____

🍃 Dinner

_____
_____
_____
_____
_____

🧁 Snack

_____
_____
_____
_____

Water Intake

[ ] [ ] [ ] [ ] [ ] [ ] [ ] [ ] [ ]

Hunger Scale

1 2 3 4 5 6 7 8 9 10
starving   So Full

I Ate Because

☐ STARVING   ☐ CRAVINGS   ☐ TROUBLED   ☐ MOODY   ☐ NEED FUEL

Symptoms/Feelings Post Meal ⟶ How Long After Meal?

☐ STRONG   ☐ BLOATING   ☐ DIGESTIVE   ☐ < 1HOUR   ☐ 1 - 2 HOURS

☐ FOCUSED   ☐ FOGGY MIND ☐ OTHER _____

what? where? When? Why?

Do I give myself enough credit? _____
_____
_____
_____
_____
_____

Date: _____ Sleep Time: _____ 😄 🙂 😐 ☹️ 😣

☕ Breakfast

_____
_____
_____
_____
_____

🌮 Lunch

_____
_____
_____
_____
_____

🍲 Dinner

_____
_____
_____
_____
_____

🧁 Snack

_____
_____
_____
_____
_____

Water Intake

🥛 🥛 🥛 🥛 🥛 🥛 🥛 🥛 🥛

Hunger Scale

1 2 3 4 5 6 7 8 9 10

starving   So Full

I Ate Because

☐ STARVING ☐ CRAVINGS ☐ TROUBLED ☐ MOODY ☐ NEED FUEL

Symptoms/Feelings Post Meal ──────➤ How Long After Meal?

☐ STRONG ☐ BLOATING ☐ DIGESTIVE ☐ < 1HOUR ☐ 1 - 2 HOURS

☐ FOCUSED ☐ FOGGY MIND ☐ OTHER _____

what? where? When? Why?

What steps can I take to eliminate anxiety (about food)? _____

_____
_____
_____
_____
_____

Date: _____ Sleep Time: _____ 😄 ☺ 😐 ☹ 😣

☕ Breakfast   🌮 Lunch   🥗 Dinner

_____   _____   _____
_____   _____   _____
_____   _____   _____
_____   _____   _____
_____   _____   _____

🧁 Snack   ──── Water Intake ────

_____   [glass] [glass] [glass] [glass] [glass] [glass] [glass] [glass] [glass]
_____
_____   ──── Hunger Scale ────
_____
_____   1 2 3 4 5 6 7 8 9 10
_____ |—————————————————————————|
                       starving   So Full

──── I Ate Because ────

☐ STARVING   ☐ CRAVINGS   ☐ TROUBLED   ☐ MOODY   ☐ NEED FUEL

┌ Symptoms/Feelings Post Meal ──────→ How Long After Meal? ┐

☐ STRONG   ☐ BLOATING   ☐ DIGESTIVE   ☐ < 1HOUR   ☐ 1- 2 HOURS

☐ FOCUSED   ☐ FOGGY MIND ☐ OTHER ──────────────────────

what? where? When? Why?

Have I had a negative food diet experience? _____

_____
_____
_____
_____
_____

Date: _____ Sleep Time: _____ 😄 🙂 😐 🙁 😣

Breakfast
_____
_____
_____
_____
_____

Lunch
_____
_____
_____
_____
_____

Dinner
_____
_____
_____
_____
_____

Snack
_____
_____
_____
_____

Water Intake

Hunger Scale

1 2 3 4 5 6 7 8 9 10

starving   So Full

I Ate Because

☐ STARVING   ☐ CRAVINGS   ☐ TROUBLED   ☐ MOODY   ☐ NEED FUEL

Symptoms/Feelings Post Meal ➞ How Long After Meal?

☐ STRONG   ☐ BLOATING   ☐ DIGESTIVE   ☐ < 1HOUR   ☐ 1 - 2 HOURS

☐ FOCUSED   ☐ FOGGY MIND   ☐ OTHER _____

what? where? When? Why?

What is my last mistake and what did you learn from it? _____
_____
_____
_____
_____
_____

Date: _____ Sleep Time: _____ 😁 🙂 😐 🙁 😣

☕ Breakfast   🌮 Lunch   🍲 Dinner

_____   _____   _____
_____   _____   _____
_____   _____   _____
_____   _____   _____
_____   _____   _____

🧁 Snack

_____

_____ Water Intake _____

[🥛 🥛 🥛 🥛 🥛 🥛 🥛 🥛 🥛]

_____

_____   _____ Hunger Scale _____

_____   1 2 3 4 5 6 7 8 9 10
_____
_____   starving   So Full

_____ I Ate Because _____

☐ STARVING   ☐ CRAVINGS   ☐ TROUBLED   ☐ MOODY   ☐ NEED FUEL

— Symptoms/Feelings Post Meal ———➤ How Long After Meal? —

☐ STRONG   ☐ BLOATING   ☐ DIGESTIVE   ☐ < 1HOUR   ☐ 1 - 2 HOURS

☐ FOCUSED   ☐ FOGGY MIND   ☐ OTHER _____

what? where? When? Why?

When I feel emotional pain, what are five things I can do for myself?

- _____
- _____
- _____
- _____
- _____

Date: _____ Sleep Time: _____ 😄 🙂 😐 🙁 😫

☕ Breakfast
_____
_____
_____
_____
_____

🥙 Lunch
_____
_____
_____
_____
_____

🍃 Dinner
_____
_____
_____
_____
_____

🧁 Snack
_____
_____
_____
_____

Water Intake
🥛 🥛 🥛 🥛 🥛 🥛 🥛 🥛 🥛

Hunger Scale
1 2 3 4 5 6 7 8 9 10
starving   So Full

I Ate Because
☐ STARVING   ☐ CRAVINGS   ☐ TROUBLED   ☐ MOODY   ☐ NEED FUEL

Symptoms/Feelings Post Meal ⟶ How Long After Meal?
☐ STRONG   ☐ BLOATING   ☐ DIGESTIVE   ☐ < 1HOUR   ☐ 1 - 2 HOURS
☐ FOCUSED   ☐ FOGGY MIND   ☐ OTHER _____

what? where? When? Why?

If I can talk to myself a year ago, the only thing I want to say is _____
_____
_____
_____
_____

Date: _____ Sleep Time: _____ 😄 🙂 😐 🙁 😣

☕ Breakfast   🌮 Lunch   🍲 Dinner

_____   _____   _____
_____   _____   _____
_____   _____   _____
_____   _____   _____
_____   _____   _____

🧁 Snack

_____

_____

_____

_____

Water Intake

Hunger Scale

| 1 | 2 | 3 | 4 | 5 | 6 | 7 | 8 | 9 | 10 |

starving   So Full

I Ate Because

☐ STARVING   ☐ CRAVINGS   ☐ TROUBLED   ☐ MOODY   ☐ NEED FUEL

Symptoms/Feelings Post Meal → How Long After Meal?

☐ STRONG   ☐ BLOATING   ☐ DIGESTIVE   ☐ < 1HOUR   ☐ 1 - 2 HOURS

☐ FOCUSED   ☐ FOGGY MIND   ☐ OTHER _____

what? where? When? Why?

What are my five major strengths? _____

_____

_____

_____

_____

_____

Date: _____ Sleep Time: _____ 😄 ☺ 😐 🙁 😣

☕ Breakfast   🌮 Lunch   🍽 Dinner

_____   _____   _____
_____   _____   _____
_____   _____   _____
_____   _____   _____

🧁 Snack

_____

_____

_____

_____

Water Intake

[ ] [ ] [ ] [ ] [ ] [ ] [ ] [ ] [ ]

Hunger Scale

1   2   3   4   5   6   7   8   9   10

starving   So Full

I Ate Because

[ ] STARVING   [ ] CRAVINGS   [ ] TROUBLED   [ ] MOODY   [ ] NEED FUEL

Symptoms/Feelings Post Meal ➡ How Long After Meal?

[ ] STRONG   [ ] BLOATING   [ ] DIGESTIVE   [ ] < 1HOUR   [ ] 1 - 2 HOURS

[ ] FOCUSED   [ ] FOGGY MIND   [ ] OTHER _____

what? where? When? Why?

Today while eating (dinner), Am I busy or calm? _____

_____

_____

_____

_____

Date: _____ Sleep Time: _____ 😄 🙂 😐 🙁 😣

☕ Breakfast

_____
_____
_____
_____
_____

🌮 Lunch

_____
_____
_____
_____
_____

🍲 Dinner

_____
_____
_____
_____
_____

🧁 Snack

_____
_____
_____
_____

Water Intake

[glass] [glass] [glass] [glass] [glass] [glass] [glass] [glass] [glass]

Hunger Scale

1 2 3 4 5 6 7 8 9 10

starving   So Full

I Ate Because

☐ STARVING   ☐ CRAVINGS   ☐ TROUBLED   ☐ MOODY   ☐ NEED FUEL

Symptoms/Feelings Post Meal ⟶ How Long After Meal?

☐ STRONG   ☐ BLOATING   ☐ DIGESTIVE   ☐ < 1HOUR   ☐ 1 - 2 HOURS

☐ FOCUSED   ☐ FOGGY MIND   ☐ OTHER _____

what? where? When? Why?

I feel stress when _____

_____
_____
_____
_____
_____

Date: _____ Sleep Time: _____ 😄 ☺ 😐 ☹ 😣

☕ **Breakfast**

_____
_____
_____
_____
_____

🌮 **Lunch**

_____
_____
_____
_____
_____

🍽 **Dinner**

_____
_____
_____
_____
_____

🧁 **Snack**

_____
_____
_____
_____

Water Intake

🥛 🥛 🥛 🥛 🥛 🥛 🥛 🥛 🥛

Hunger Scale

| 1 | 2 | 3 | 4 | 5 | 6 | 7 | 8 | 9 | 10 |

starving   So Full

I Ate Because

☐ STARVING ☐ CRAVINGS ☐ TROUBLED ☐ MOODY ☐ NEED FUEL

Symptoms/Feelings Post Meal ⟶ **How Long After Meal?**

☐ STRONG ☐ BLOATING ☐ DIGESTIVE ☐ < 1HOUR ☐ 1 - 2 HOURS

☐ FOCUSED ☐ FOGGY MIND ☐ OTHER _____

what? where? When? Why?

Do I easily feel frustrated or angry when I am not achieving my goals?

_____
_____
_____
_____

Date: _____ Sleep Time: _____ 😄 ☺ 😐 ☹ 😫

☕ Breakfast   🌮 Lunch   🍜 Dinner

_____   _____   _____
_____   _____   _____
_____   _____   _____
_____   _____   _____
_____   _____   _____

🧁 Snack   Water Intake
_____   ▢ ▢ ▢ ▢ ▢ ▢ ▢ ▢ ▢
_____
_____   Hunger Scale
_____   1 2 3 4 5 6 7 8 9 10
_____   starving   So Full

_____ I Ate Because _____
☐ STARVING   ☐ CRAVINGS   ☐ TROUBLED   ☐ MOODY   ☐ NEED FUEL

— Symptoms/Feelings Post Meal ——→ How Long After Meal? —
☐ STRONG   ☐ BLOATING   ☐ DIGESTIVE   ☐ < 1HOUR   ☐ 1 - 2 HOURS
☐ FOCUSED   ☐ FOGGY MIND   ☐ OTHER _____

what? where? When? Why?

Deep inside, do I know that there is more than one way to achieve
a better outcome? _____

_____
_____
_____
_____

Date: _____ Sleep Time: _____ 😁 🙂 😐 🙁 😖

☕ Breakfast

_____
_____
_____
_____
_____

🌮 Lunch

_____
_____
_____
_____
_____

🍝 Dinner

_____
_____
_____
_____
_____

🧁 Snack

_____
_____
_____
_____

Water Intake

🥛 🥛 🥛 🥛 🥛 🥛 🥛 🥛 🥛

Hunger Scale

1 2 3 4 5 6 7 8 9 10

starving   So Full

I Ate Because

☐ STARVING ☐ CRAVINGS ☐ TROUBLED ☐ MOODY ☐ NEED FUEL

Symptoms/Feelings Post Meal ⟶ How Long After Meal?

☐ STRONG ☐ BLOATING ☐ DIGESTIVE   ☐ < 1HOUR ☐ 1 - 2 HOURS

☐ FOCUSED ☐ FOGGY MIND ☐ OTHER _____

what? where? When? Why?

What are things that really important to me? _____

_____
_____
_____
_____
_____

Date: _____ Sleep Time: _____ 😄 ☺ 😐 ☹ 😣

☕ Breakfast   🌮 Lunch   🍲 Dinner

_____   _____   _____
_____   _____   _____
_____   _____   _____
_____   _____   _____
_____   _____   _____

🧁 Snack

_____

Water Intake

_____   _____   _____
_____

Hunger Scale

1   2   3   4   5   6   7   8   9   10

starving   So Full

I Ate Because

☐ STARVING   ☐ CRAVINGS   ☐ TROUBLED   ☐ MOODY   ☐ NEED FUEL

Symptoms/Feelings Post Meal ➡ How Long After Meal?

☐ STRONG   ☐ BLOATING   ☐ DIGESTIVE   ☐ < 1HOUR   ☐ 1 - 2 HOURS

☐ FOCUSED   ☐ FOGGY MIND   ☐ OTHER _____

what? where? When? Why?

What are the things I am proud of in my life so far? _____

_____

_____

_____

_____

_____

Date: _____ Sleep Time: _____ 😄 ☺ 😐 ☹ 😖

☕ Breakfast   🌮 Lunch   🍽 Dinner

_____   _____   _____
_____   _____   _____
_____   _____   _____
_____   _____   _____
_____   _____   _____

🧁 Snack

_____

_____

_____

_____

_____

Water Intake

▯ ▯ ▯ ▯ ▯ ▯ ▯ ▯ ▯

Hunger Scale

1　2　3　4　5　6　7　8　9　10

starving   So Full

I Ate Because

☐ STARVING ☐ CRAVINGS ☐ TROUBLED ☐ MOODY ☐ NEED FUEL

Symptoms/Feelings Post Meal ⟶ How Long After Meal?

☐ STRONG ☐ BLOATING ☐ DIGESTIVE ☐ < 1HOUR ☐ 1 - 2 HOURS

☐ FOCUSED ☐ FOGGY MIND ☐ OTHER _____

what? where? When? Why?

Which of my talents or skills gives me the greatest sense of pride
or satisfaction? _____

_____

_____

_____

_____

Date: _____   Sleep Time: _____   😄 ☺ 😐 ☹ 😣

☕ Breakfast   🌮 Lunch   🍲 Dinner

_____   _____   _____
_____   _____   _____
_____   _____   _____
_____   _____   _____
_____   _____   _____

🧁 Snack   ———— Water Intake ————

_____   🥛 🥛 🥛 🥛 🥛 🥛 🥛 🥛 🥛
_____
_____   ———— Hunger Scale ————
_____
_____   1 2 3 4 5 6 7 8 9 10
                    starving   So Full

———— I Ate Because ————

☐ STARVING   ☐ CRAVINGS   ☐ TROUBLED   ☐ MOODY   ☐ NEED FUEL

— Symptoms/Feelings Post Meal ——➤ How Long After Meal? —

☐ STRONG   ☐ BLOATING   ☐ DIGESTIVE   ☐ < 1HOUR   ☐ 1 - 2 HOURS

☐ FOCUSED   ☐ FOGGY MIND ☐ OTHER _____

what? where? When? Why?

I feel happier in my skin when _____
_____
_____
_____
_____
_____

Date: _____ Sleep Time: _____ 😄 🙂 😐 🙁 😣

☕ Breakfast

_____
_____
_____
_____

🌮 Lunch

_____
_____
_____
_____

🍃 Dinner

_____
_____
_____
_____

🧁 Snack

_____
_____
_____
_____

Water Intake

🥛 🥛 🥛 🥛 🥛 🥛 🥛 🥛 🥛

Hunger Scale

1   2   3   4   5   6   7   8   9   10

starving   So Full

I Ate Because

☐ STARVING ☐ CRAVINGS ☐ TROUBLED ☐ MOODY ☐ NEED FUEL

Symptoms/Feelings Post Meal ⟶ How Long After Meal?

☐ STRONG ☐ BLOATING ☐ DIGESTIVE ☐ < 1HOUR ☐ 1 - 2 HOURS

☐ FOCUSED ☐ FOGGY MIND ☐ OTHER _____

what? where? When? Why?

My favorite way to spend the day is _____
_____
_____
_____
_____

Date: _____ Sleep Time: _____ 😄 🙂 😐 🙁 😣

☕ Breakfast

_____
_____
_____
_____

🌮 Lunch

_____
_____
_____
_____

🍽 Dinner

_____
_____
_____
_____

🧁 Snack

_____
_____
_____
_____

Water Intake

🥛 🥛 🥛 🥛 🥛 🥛 🥛 🥛 🥛

Hunger Scale

1   2   3   4   5   6   7   8   9   10
starving   So Full

I Ate Because

☐ STARVING   ☐ CRAVINGS   ☐ TROUBLED   ☐ MOODY   ☐ NEED FUEL

Symptoms/Feelings Post Meal ⟶ How Long After Meal?

☐ STRONG   ☐ BLOATING   ☐ DIGESTIVE   ☐ < 1HOUR   ☐ 1 - 2 HOURS

☐ FOCUSED   ☐ FOGGY MIND   ☐ OTHER _____

what? where? When? Why?

How much do I trust myself? _____

_____
_____
_____
_____
_____

Date: _____ Sleep Time: _____ 😄 🙂 😐 🙁 😣

Breakfast

_____
_____
_____
_____
_____

Lunch

_____
_____
_____
_____
_____

Dinner

_____
_____
_____
_____
_____

Snack

_____
_____
_____
_____
_____

Water Intake

☐ ☐ ☐ ☐ ☐ ☐ ☐ ☐ ☐

Hunger Scale

1 2 3 4 5 6 7 8 9 10

starving   So Full

I Ate Because

☐ STARVING ☐ CRAVINGS ☐ TROUBLED ☐ MOODY ☐ NEED FUEL

Symptoms/Feelings Post Meal ⟶ How Long After Meal?

☐ STRONG ☐ BLOATING ☐ DIGESTIVE ☐ < 1HOUR ☐ 1 - 2 HOURS

☐ FOCUSED ☐ FOGGY MIND ☐ OTHER _____

what? where? When? Why?

What are some tough questions about my health? _____
_____
_____
_____
_____
_____

Date: _____ Sleep Time: _____ 😁 ☺ 😐 ☹ 😫

☕ Breakfast   🌮 Lunch   🍲 Dinner

_____   _____   _____
_____   _____   _____
_____   _____   _____
_____   _____   _____
_____   _____   _____

🧁 Snack

_____
_____
_____
_____
_____

Water Intake _____

☐ ☐ ☐ ☐ ☐ ☐ ☐ ☐ ☐

Hunger Scale

1   2   3   4   5   6   7   8   9   10

starving   So Full

I Ate Because

☐ STARVING   ☐ CRAVINGS   ☐ TROUBLED   ☐ MOODY   ☐ NEED FUEL

Symptoms/Feelings Post Meal ➔ How Long After Meal?

☐ STRONG   ☐ BLOATING   ☐ DIGESTIVE   ☐ < 1HOUR   ☐ 1 - 2 HOURS

☐ FOCUSED   ☐ FOGGY MIND   ☐ OTHER _____

what? where? When? Why?

Am I willing to ask for the support I need? _____

_____
_____
_____
_____
_____

Date: _____ Sleep Time: _____ 😁 🙂 😐 🙁 😣

☕ Breakfast   🍞 Lunch   🍽 Dinner

_____   _____   _____
_____   _____   _____
_____   _____   _____
_____   _____   _____

🧁 Snack

_____
_____
_____
_____

Water Intake

▯ ▯ ▯ ▯ ▯ ▯ ▯ ▯ ▯

Hunger Scale

1   2   3   4   5   6   7   8   9   10

starving   So Full

I Ate Because

☐ STARVING   ☐ CRAVINGS   ☐ TROUBLED   ☐ MOODY   ☐ NEED FUEL

Symptoms/Feelings Post Meal ➝ How Long After Meal?

☐ STRONG   ☐ BLOATING   ☐ DIGESTIVE   ☐ < 1HOUR   ☐ 1 - 2 HOURS

☐ FOCUSED   ☐ FOGGY MIND   ☐ OTHER _____

what? where? When? Why?

What are my greatest talents or skills? _____

_____
_____
_____
_____
_____

Date: _____ Sleep Time: _____ 😄 🙂 😐 🙁 😣

☕ Breakfast   🌮 Lunch   🍲 Dinner

_____   _____   _____
_____   _____   _____
_____   _____   _____
_____   _____   _____

🧁 Snack

_____

____ Water Intake ____

[glass] [glass] [glass] [glass] [glass] [glass] [glass] [glass] [glass]

_____

_____   ____ Hunger Scale ____

_____   1 2 3 4 5 6 7 8 9 10
                      starving   So Full

____ I Ate Because ____

☐ STARVING   ☐ CRAVINGS   ☐ TROUBLED   ☐ MOODY   ☐ NEED FUEL

┌ Symptoms/Feelings Post Meal ──────➤ How Long After Meal? ┐

☐ STRONG   ☐ BLOATING   ☐ DIGESTIVE   ☐ < 1HOUR   ☐ 1 - 2 HOURS

☐ FOCUSED   ☐ FOGGY MIND   ☐ OTHER _____

what? where? When? Why?

What would I like to stop worrying about? _____

_____
_____
_____
_____
_____

Date: _____ Sleep Time: _____ 😁 🙂 😐 🙁 😣

☕ Breakfast   🌮 Lunch   🍽 Dinner

_____   _____   _____
_____   _____   _____
_____   _____   _____
_____   _____   _____
_____   _____   _____

🧁 Snack

_____   ── Water Intake ──
_____   [🥛] [🥛] [🥛] [🥛] [🥛] [🥛] [🥛] [🥛] [🥛]
_____
_____   ── Hunger Scale ──
_____   1 2 3 4 5 6 7 8 9 10
                   starving   So Full

── I Ate Because ──
☐ STARVING ☐ CRAVINGS ☐ TROUBLED ☐ MOODY ☐ NEED FUEL

── Symptoms/Feelings Post Meal ──➤ How Long After Meal? ──
☐ STRONG   ☐ BLOATING   ☐ DIGESTIVE   ☐ < 1HOUR ☐ 1 - 2 HOURS
☐ FOCUSED   ☐ FOGGY MIND ☐ OTHER _____

what? where? When? Why?

What's one thing I would like to do more of and why? How can I make
that happen? _____
_____
_____
_____
_____

Date: _____   Sleep Time: _____   😁 🙂 😐 ☹️ 😣

☕ Breakfast

_____
_____
_____
_____

🌮 Lunch

_____
_____
_____
_____

🍝 Dinner

_____
_____
_____
_____

🧁 Snack

_____
_____
_____
_____

Water Intake

🥛 🥛 🥛 🥛 🥛 🥛 🥛 🥛 🥛

Hunger Scale

1 2 3 4 5 6 7 8 9 10

starving   So Full

I Ate Because

☐ STARVING   ☐ CRAVINGS   ☐ TROUBLED   ☐ MOODY   ☐ NEED FUEL

Symptoms/Feelings Post Meal ———→ How Long After Meal?

☐ STRONG   ☐ BLOATING   ☐ DIGESTIVE   ☐ < 1HOUR   ☐ 1 - 2 HOURS

☐ FOCUSED   ☐ FOGGY MIND   ☐ OTHER _____

what? where? When? Why?

Which five words describe me best? _____

_____
_____
_____
_____
_____

Date:_____ Sleep Time:_____ 😄 ☺ 😐 ☹ 😫

☕ **Breakfast**   🌮 **Lunch**   🥗 **Dinner**

_____   _____   _____
_____   _____   _____
_____   _____   _____
_____   _____   _____
_____   _____   _____

🧁 **Snack**

_____

_____

_____

_____

_____ **Water Intake** _____

[ ] [ ] [ ] [ ] [ ] [ ] [ ] [ ] [ ]

_____ **Hunger Scale** _____

1   2   3   4   5   6   7   8   9   10

starving   So Full

_____ **I Ate Because** _____

[ ] STARVING [ ] CRAVINGS [ ] TROUBLED [ ] MOODY [ ] NEED FUEL

— **Symptoms/Feelings Post Meal** ——→ **How Long After Meal?** —

[ ] STRONG   [ ] BLOATING   [ ] DIGESTIVE   [ ] < 1HOUR   [ ] 1 - 2 HOURS

[ ] FOCUSED [ ] FOGGY MIND [ ] OTHER _____

what? where? When? Why?

What are my most important needs and desires? _____

_____

_____

_____

_____

Date: _____   Sleep Time: _____   😄 🙂 😐 🙁 😣

☕ Breakfast   🌮 Lunch   🍝 Dinner
_____   _____   _____
_____   _____   _____
_____   _____   _____
_____   _____   _____
_____   _____   _____

🧁 Snack   ——— Water Intake ———
_____   [🥛 🥛 🥛 🥛 🥛 🥛 🥛 🥛 🥛]
_____
_____   ——— Hunger Scale ———
_____   1 2 3 4 5 6 7 8 9 10
_____   starving   So Full

——— I Ate Because ———
☐ STARVING   ☐ CRAVINGS   ☐ TROUBLED   ☐ MOODY   ☐ NEED FUEL

Symptoms/Feelings Post Meal ——▶ How Long After Meal?
☐ STRONG   ☐ BLOATING   ☐ DIGESTIVE   ☐ < 1HOUR   ☐ 1 - 2 HOURS
☐ FOCUSED   ☐ FOGGY MIND ☐ OTHER _____

what? where? When? Why?

What are my personal gifts? _____
_____
_____
_____
_____
_____

Date: _____ Sleep Time: _____ 😁 ☺ 😐 ☹ 😣

☕ Breakfast   🌮 Lunch   🍽 Dinner

_____   _____   _____
_____   _____   _____
_____   _____   _____
_____   _____   _____
_____   _____   _____

🧁 Snack

_____

_____

_____

_____

Water Intake

Hunger Scale

1   2   3   4   5   6   7   8   9   10

starving   So Full

I Ate Because

☐ STARVING   ☐ CRAVINGS   ☐ TROUBLED   ☐ MOODY   ☐ NEED FUEL

Symptoms/Feelings Post Meal ➡ How Long After Meal?

☐ STRONG   ☐ BLOATING   ☐ DIGESTIVE   ☐ < 1HOUR   ☐ 1 - 2 HOURS

☐ FOCUSED   ☐ FOGGY MIND   ☐ OTHER _____

what? where? When? Why?

When do I think about eating? _____

_____

_____

_____

_____

_____

Date: _____ Sleep Time: _____ 😁 🙂 😐 🙁 😣

☕ Breakfast   🌮 Lunch   🥗 Dinner
_____   _____   _____
_____   _____   _____
_____   _____   _____
_____   _____   _____

🧁 Snack   _____ Water Intake _____
_____   [glass][glass][glass][glass][glass][glass][glass][glass][glass]
_____
_____   _____ Hunger Scale _____
_____   1 2 3 4 5 6 7 8 9 10
                          starving   So Full

_____ I Ate Because _____
☐ STARVING ☐ CRAVINGS ☐ TROUBLED ☐ MOODY ☐ NEED FUEL

Symptoms/Feelings Post Meal ⟶ How Long After Meal?
☐ STRONG ☐ BLOATING ☐ DIGESTIVE ☐ < 1HOUR ☐ 1 - 2 HOURS
☐ FOCUSED ☐ FOGGY MIND ☐ OTHER

what? where? When? Why?

When do I decide to eat? _____
_____
_____
_____
_____

Date: _____ Sleep Time: _____ 😄 ☺ 😐 ☹ 😖

☕ Breakfast

_____
_____
_____
_____
_____

🌮 Lunch

_____
_____
_____
_____
_____

🍤 Dinner

_____
_____
_____
_____
_____

🧁 Snack

_____
_____
_____
_____

Water Intake

🥛 🥛 🥛 🥛 🥛 🥛 🥛 🥛 🥛

Hunger Scale

1	2	3	4	5	6	7	8	9	10

starving   So Full

I Ate Because

☐ STARVING   ☐ CRAVINGS   ☐ TROUBLED   ☐ MOODY   ☐ NEED FUEL

Symptoms/Feelings Post Meal ➔ How Long After Meal?

☐ STRONG   ☐ BLOATING   ☐ DIGESTIVE   ☐ < 1HOUR   ☐ 1 - 2 HOURS

☐ FOCUSED   ☐ FOGGY MIND   ☐ OTHER _____

what? where? When? Why?

What should I do to get more peace in my life? _____
_____
_____
_____
_____
_____

Date: _____ Sleep Time: _____ 😄 ☺ 😐 ☹ 😖

☕ Breakfast   🌮 Lunch   🍽 Dinner

_____   _____   _____
_____   _____   _____
_____   _____   _____
_____   _____   _____
_____   _____   _____

🧁 Snack   ———— Water Intake ————

_____   🥛 🥛 🥛 🥛 🥛 🥛 🥛 🥛 🥛
_____
_____   ———— Hunger Scale ————
_____
_____   1 2 3 4 5 6 7 8 9 10
                          starving   So Full

———— I Ate Because ————

☐ STARVING   ☐ CRAVINGS   ☐ TROUBLED   ☐ MOODY   ☐ NEED FUEL

— Symptoms/Feelings Post Meal ——→ How Long After Meal? —

☐ STRONG   ☐ BLOATING   ☐ DIGESTIVE   ☐ < 1HOUR   ☐ 1 - 2 HOURS

☐ FOCUSED   ☐ FOGGY MIND ☐ OTHER _____

what? where? When? Why?

What do I "eat" choose from all the available options? _____

_____
_____
_____
_____
_____

Date: _____ Sleep Time: _____ 😄 🙂 😐 🙁 😣

☕ Breakfast   🌮 Lunch   🍝 Dinner

_____ _____ _____
_____ _____ _____
_____ _____ _____
_____ _____ _____
_____ _____ _____

🧁 Snack

_____

_____

_____

_____

—————— Water Intake ——————

▯ ▯ ▯ ▯ ▯ ▯ ▯ ▯ ▯

—————— Hunger Scale ——————

1 2 3 4 5 6 7 8 9 10

starving   So Full

—————— I Ate Because ——————

☐ STARVING ☐ CRAVINGS ☐ TROUBLED ☐ MOODY ☐ NEED FUEL

Symptoms/Feelings Post Meal ⟶ How Long After Meal?

☐ STRONG ☐ BLOATING ☐ DIGESTIVE   ☐ < 1HOUR ☐ 1 - 2 HOURS

☐ FOCUSED ☐ FOGGY MIND ☐ OTHER _____

what? where? When? Why?

Where does the fuel I have consumed go? _____

_____

_____

_____

_____

_____

Date: _____ Sleep Time: _____ 😄 ☺ 😐 🙁 😣

☕ Breakfast   🌮 Lunch   🍵 Dinner

_____   _____   _____
_____   _____   _____
_____   _____   _____
_____   _____   _____
_____   _____   _____

🧁 Snack

_____   ———— Water Intake ————
_____   [glass] [glass] [glass] [glass] [glass] [glass] [glass] [glass] [glass]
_____
_____   ———— Hunger Scale ————
_____   1 2 3 4 5 6 7 8 9 10
                    starving   So Full

———— I Ate Because ————

☐ STARVING   ☐ CRAVINGS   ☐ TROUBLED   ☐ MOODY   ☐ NEED FUEL

— Symptoms/Feelings Post Meal ——→ How Long After Meal? —

☐ STRONG   ☐ BLOATING   ☐ DIGESTIVE   ☐ < 1HOUR   ☐ 1 - 2 HOURS

☐ FOCUSED   ☐ FOGGY MIND   ☐ OTHER _____

what? where? When? Why?

Am I living my passion? _____

_____
_____
_____
_____
_____

Date: _____ Sleep Time: _____ 😄 ☺ 😐 ☹ 😣

☕ Breakfast

_____
_____
_____
_____
_____

🌮 Lunch

_____
_____
_____
_____
_____

🍤 Dinner

_____
_____
_____
_____
_____

🧁 Snack

_____
_____
_____
_____
_____

_____ Water Intake _____

🥛 🥛 🥛 🥛 🥛 🥛 🥛 🥛 🥛

_____ Hunger Scale _____

1 2 3 4 5 6 7 8 9 10

starving   So Full

_____ I Ate Because _____

☐ STARVING ☐ CRAVINGS ☐ TROUBLED ☐ MOODY ☐ NEED FUEL

Symptoms/Feelings Post Meal ⟶ How Long After Meal?

☐ STRONG ☐ BLOATING ☐ DIGESTIVE ☐ < 1HOUR ☐ 1 - 2 HOURS

☐ FOCUSED ☐ FOGGY MIND ☐ OTHER _____

what? where? When? Why?

Is my worst-case scenario really likely to happen? _____
_____
_____
_____
_____

Date: _____ Sleep Time: _____ 😄 ☺ 😐 ☹ 😫

☕ Breakfast   🌮 Lunch   🍤 Dinner

_____   _____   _____
_____   _____   _____
_____   _____   _____
_____   _____   _____
_____   _____   _____

🧁 Snack

_____

—————————— Water Intake ——————————

[glass] [glass] [glass] [glass] [glass] [glass] [glass] [glass] [glass]

—————————— Hunger Scale ——————————

1   2   3   4   5   6   7   8   9   10

starving   So Full

———————————— I Ate Because ————————————

☐ STARVING   ☐ CRAVINGS   ☐ TROUBLED   ☐ MOODY   ☐ NEED FUEL

— Symptoms/Feelings Post Meal ——→ How Long After Meal? —

☐ STRONG   ☐ BLOATING   ☐ DIGESTIVE   ☐ < 1HOUR   ☐ 1 - 2 HOURS

☐ FOCUSED   ☐ FOGGY MIND   ☐ OTHER _____

what? where? When? Why?

When was the last time I had a good laugh? _____

_____
_____
_____
_____
_____

Date: _____ Sleep Time: _____ 😄 ☺ 😐 🙁 😣

Breakfast

_____
_____
_____
_____
_____
_____

Lunch

_____
_____
_____
_____
_____
_____

Dinner

_____
_____
_____
_____
_____
_____

Snack

_____
_____
_____
_____

Water Intake

Hunger Scale

| 1 | 2 | 3 | 4 | 5 | 6 | 7 | 8 | 9 | 10 |

starving   So Full

I Ate Because

☐ STARVING   ☐ CRAVINGS   ☐ TROUBLED   ☐ MOODY   ☐ NEED FUEL

Symptoms/Feelings Post Meal ⟶ How Long After Meal?

☐ STRONG   ☐ BLOATING   ☐ DIGESTIVE   ☐ < 1HOUR   ☐ 1 - 2 HOURS

☐ FOCUSED   ☐ FOGGY MIND   ☐ OTHER _____

what? where? When? Why?

What would I be risking if I did some of the things that are outside
of my comfort zone? _____

_____
_____
_____
_____

Date: _____ Sleep Time: _____ 😄 🙂 😐 🙁 😣

☕ Breakfast   🌮 Lunch   🥗 Dinner

_____   _____   _____
_____   _____   _____
_____   _____   _____
_____   _____   _____
_____   _____   _____

🧁 Snack

_____

—————————— Water Intake ——————————

[glass][glass][glass][glass][glass][glass][glass][glass][glass]

_____

—————————— Hunger Scale ——————————

1 2 3 4 5 6 7 8 9 10
starving   So Full

—————————— I Ate Because ——————————

☐ STARVING   ☐ CRAVINGS   ☐ TROUBLED   ☐ MOODY   ☐ NEED FUEL

— Symptoms/Feelings Post Meal ——→ How Long After Meal? —

☐ STRONG   ☐ BLOATING   ☐ DIGESTIVE   ☐ < 1HOUR   ☐ 1 - 2 HOURS

☐ FOCUSED   ☐ FOGGY MIND   ☐ OTHER _____

what? where? When? Why?

What is the single, most significant change I can make in this year? ——

_____
_____
_____
_____
_____

Date: _____   Sleep Time: _____   😄 🙂 😐 🙁 😣

☕ Breakfast

_____
_____
_____
_____
_____

🌮 Lunch

_____
_____
_____
_____
_____

🍽 Dinner

_____
_____
_____
_____
_____

🧁 Snack

_____
_____
_____
_____

Water Intake

🥛 🥛 🥛 🥛 🥛 🥛 🥛 🥛 🥛

Hunger Scale

| 1 | 2 | 3 | 4 | 5 | 6 | 7 | 8 | 9 | 10 |

starving   So Full

I Ate Because

☐ STARVING ☐ CRAVINGS ☐ TROUBLED ☐ MOODY ☐ NEED FUEL

Symptoms/Feelings Post Meal ➡ How Long After Meal?

☐ STRONG   ☐ BLOATING   ☐ DIGESTIVE   ☐ < 1HOUR   ☐ 1 - 2 HOURS

☐ FOCUSED   ☐ FOGGY MIND ☐ OTHER _____

what? where? When? Why?

I wish I could _____
_____
_____
_____
_____
_____

Date: _____ Sleep Time: _____ 😄 ☺ 😐 ☹ 😣

☕ Breakfast   🌮 Lunch   🥗 Dinner

_____   _____   _____
_____   _____   _____
_____   _____   _____
_____   _____   _____
_____   _____   _____

🧁 Snack

_____

_____   Water Intake
_____   🥛 🥛 🥛 🥛 🥛 🥛 🥛 🥛 🥛
_____

                              Hunger Scale
                    1   2   3   4   5   6   7   8   9   10
                    starving   So Full

I Ate Because

☐ STARVING   ☐ CRAVINGS   ☐ TROUBLED   ☐ MOODY   ☐ NEED FUEL

Symptoms/Feelings Post Meal ——→ How Long After Meal?

☐ STRONG   ☐ BLOATING   ☐ DIGESTIVE   ☐ < 1HOUR   ☐ 1 - 2 HOURS

☐ FOCUSED   ☐ FOGGY MIND ☐ OTHER _____

what? where? When? Why?

One of the most important things I learned was _____

_____

_____

_____

_____

_____

I may be the only person left who believes in me, but it's enough. It takes just one star to pierce a universe of darkness, Failure will never overtake me if my determination to succeed is strong enough.
(Og Mandino -Richelle E)

	Yes	No
Did I achieve My goals	☐	☐
I will use this journal again	☐	☐
Is it worth a good review	☐	☐

Printed in Great Britain
by Amazon